The Comprehensive Book of Modes & Scales

for Piano & Keyboard Players

Copyright 2013
by
Kevin G. Pace

PaceMusicServices.com

CONTENTS

Pg #			Pg #		
1	Explanation		45	Octatonic scales	**8 TONE SCALES**
3	Ionian (major)		46	Symmetrical Augmented Scale	**6 TONE SCALE**
4	Dorian		47	Chromatic Scale	**12 TONE SCALE**
5	Phrygian		48	Gypsy (aka Byzantine or Double Harmonic Minor)	
6	Lydian	**CHURCH MODES**	49	Arabian Major	
7	Mixolydian		50	Harmonic Minor b2 (aka Balinese)	
8	Aeolian (natural minor)		51	Hungarian Gypsy	**EXOTIC SCALES**
9	Locrian		52	Persian	
10	More on Church Modes scales and chords		53	East Indian Purvi	
11	Pentatonic Mode 1 (aka Minor Pentatonic)		54	Locrian #3 (also called Oriental)	
12	Pentatonic Mode 2 (aka Major Pentatonic)		55	Synthetic Pentatonic Scales explanation	
13	Pentatonic Mode 3	**PENTATONIC SCALES**	56	Major Pentatonic b6 (flat 6)	
14	Pentatonic Mode 4		57	Major Pentatonic b3 (flat 3)	
15	Pentatonic Mode 5		58	Minor 6 (add 4) Pentatonic	
16	Bebop 7th (adds a b7 into major)	**BEBOP SCALES**	59	Half-diminished (add 4) Pentatonic	
17	Bebop Major (adds a b6 into major)		60	Lydian-Augmented Major 7 Pentatonic	
18	Blues - minor	**BLUES SCALES**	61	Minor Lydian-Augmented Major 7 Pentatonic	
19	Blues - Major		62	Lydian-Augmented (add 9) Pentatonic	
20	Whole tone	**6 TONE SCALE**	63	Half-diminished 9 Pentatonic	**5 TONE SCALES**
21	Melodic minor (Dorian #7)		64	Half-diminished b13 Pentatonic	
22	Phrygian #6 (Melodic minor mode 2)		65	Diminished 9 Pentatonic	
23	Lydian Augmented (mode 3)		66	Diminished (add 11) Pentatonic	
24	Lydian Dominant (mode 4)	**MODES OF MELODIC MINOR**	67	Diminished (#5) Pentatonic	
25	Mixolydian b6 (mode 5)		68	Diminished Major 7 Pentatonic	
26	Locrian #2 (mode 6)		69	Dominant 9 Pentatonic	
27	Altered (mode 7)		70	Pelog (Asian Pentatonic)	
28	More on Melodic Minor scales and chords		71	Hirajoshi (Asian Pentatonic)	
29	Harmonic minor (Aeolian #7)		72	Other Scale Possibilities explanation	
30	Locrian #6 (Harmonic minor mode 2)		73	Ionian b2 (flat 2)	
31	Ionian #5 (mode 3)		74	Aeolian b4 (flat 4)	**OTHER SCALES**
32	Dorian #4 (mode 4)	**MODES OF HARMONIC MINOR**	75	Bebop Dorian	
33	Phrygian #3 (mode 5)		76	Lydian Dominant b2 (flat 2)	
34	Lydian #2 (mode 6)		77	Other Interesting Scales	
35	Altered b7 (mode 7)		78	Arabian Major - mode 3 (an inverted exotic scale)	
36	More on Harmonic Minor scales and chords		79	Two Semitone Tritone (a 6-note scale)	
37	Harmonic Major (Ionian b6)		80	Major Tetrachord Octatonic (an 8-note scale)	
38	Dorian b5 (Harmonic Major mode 2)		81	Tri-Cluster Nonatonic (a 9-note scale)	
39	Phrygian b4 (mode 3)		82	Decatonic (a 10-note scale)	
40	Lydian b3 (mode 4)	**MODES OF HARMONIC MAJOR**	83	Scales to play with chords	
41	Mixolydian b2 (mode 5)		90	More on Major Pentatonic & chords	**CHORDS & SCALES**
42	Lydian Augmented #2 (mode 6)		91	More on Minor Pentatonic & chords	
43	Locrian b7 (mode 7)		92	Glossary of terms	
44	More on Harmonic Major scales and chords		94	Acknowledgements	

Explanation

Reason for this book
This book of scales was written with the intent of making many scales available and understandable to musicians. As a classically trained pianist, I was never taught anything beyond the major and minor scales. The "Church Modes" of Dorian, Phrygian, Lydian, Mixolydian, and Locrian were a mystery to me. I knew nothing of the jazz scales such as Lydian Augmented or Ionian #5. This book was written so that other musicians similarly trained without a knowledge of these wonderfully sounding scales might come to understand these scales.

Composers
This book is especially useful for composers who desire to expand their sonic palette. Like a painter discovering new, exciting color blends, these scales can give the composer many new tools and sounds for his/her compositions.

Chords
The chords listed in this book are possible chords against which certain scales can be played. For every chord, there are one or more scales that have a similar sound, that sound "good" together. They are not the only chords that can be used, but merely some common chords.

Chords are generally made by stacking thirds from the scale. For example, 2 octaves of the C Dorian scale are: C-D-Eb-F-G-A-Bb-C-D-Eb-F-G-A-Bb-C. If I want to make a C minor 9 chord, I simply start on C, and then add notes by thirds, (skipping every other note in the scale) until I've arrived at the 9th scale degree. So the C minor 9 chord is C-Eb-G-Bb-D. The C minor 13 chord uses all the notes of the Dorian Scale: C-Eb-G-Bb-D-F-A. When playing a chord with many notes, it is not necessary to play all the notes. Often only the richest sounding notes are played. You might try leaving out the 5th, 9th and 11th, so the resulting C minor 13 becomes C-Eb-Bb-A.

How to say the names of scales
Here are some examples of how to say the names of the scales: "Lydian b3", would be spoken as, "Lydian flat 3". "Locrian #6" would be spoken as "Locrian sharp 6".

Fingerings of 7 note scales
Instead of giving specific sets of fingerings, I give here some general fingering guidelines. Fingerings alternate with 1-2-3-4-1-2-3 fingerings. The 5th finger is used only at the beginning or end of a scale. For example, when playing a G Ionian (Major) scale one could use the following fingerings:

RH	1	2	3	1	2	3	4	1	2	3	1	2	3	4	5
	G	A	B	C	D	E	F#	G	A	B	C	D	E	F#	G
LH	5	4	3	2	1	3	2	1	4	3	2	1	3	2	1

Notice the repeating pattern of 1-2-3-4-1-2-3. Fingerings are the same up or down.

Use of thumbs

Generally, don't play a black key with your thumb, unless the scale is made up of only black keys, like Eb Pentatonic Mode 1. It is often useful to cross your thumb right after a black key or cross a 3rd or 4th finger over a thumb.

Study the following example of Eb major:

RH	3	1	2	3	4	1	2	3	1	2	3	4	1	2	3
	Eb	F	G	Ab	Bb	C	D	Eb	F	G	Ab	Bb	C	D	Eb
LH	3	2	1	4	3	2	1	3	2	1	4	3	2	1	3

Play the above Eb Major scale and notice that the right hand thumb crosses under the Eb and again after the Bb in the ascending scale. In the descending scale, the 4 crosses over the thumb to the black key Bb, then the 3 crosses over the thumb to the black key Eb. Similar crossings occur in the LH. This really sums up the fingerings in most of the seven note scales. So, the only challenge is to figure out which finger to start on. With a little experimenting, this can be quickly determined.

Which finger to start on?

It depends on where the black keys are. You need to find a recurring finger pattern that works. For instance, if a scale starts with three black keys then start with RH 2 or LH 4. Remember you will alternate crossing 3 or 4 over the thumb or the thumb under after the 3 or 4. In other words, if you have used 1-2-3-4, then you will next use 1-2-3. If that doesn't work, try starting on another finger until you find one that works. Looking again at the Eb major scale, the RH finger started at 3, then 1-2-3-4, then 1-2-3, then 1-2-3-4, then 1-2-3. Most scales have this recurring pattern.

For fingerings of non-seven note scales, see individual scales in this book.

Fingerings of the Octatonic Scales:

RH	1	2	3	1	3	1	2	3	1	2	3	1	3	1	2	3	1
	C	Db	Eb	E	F#	G	A	Bb	C	Db	Eb	E	F#	G	A	Bb	C
LH	1	3	2	1	3	2	1	3	1	3	2	1	3	2	1	3	1

Because of the recurring whole step, half step pattern, only fingers 1, 2, and 3 are used. If the Octatonic scale starts on a note other than C, just start with the finger on this chart that corresponds to the starting note. For example, if it starts on Db, start with RH 2.

Abbreviations you may see in this book:

M2=Major 2nd, m2=minor 2nd, M3=Major 3rd, m3=minor 3rd, P4=Perfect 4th, P5=Perfect 5th, M6=Major 6th, m6=minor 6th, Tonic=scale degree #1.

I hope you enjoy this book and also find it useful.

Copyright 2013 by
Kevin G. Pace (PaceMusicServices.com)

Ionian (Major)

The Ionian Mode is commonly called the major scale

Interesting or defining features:
Minor 2nds between scale degrees 3 & 4, 7 & 8

Chords that may be used with this scale: (examples in C Ionian)
Major triad (C-E-G)   Major 6 (C-E-G-A)
Major 7 (C-E-G-B)   Major 9 (C-E-G-B-D)
Major 13 (C-E-G-B-D-A)

Here are two ways to think about the Ionian scale:
1-Think of its intervals
    For example: W   W   H   W   W   W   H
        W=Whole step or 2 half steps
        H=Half step

2-Two tetrachords hooked together by a half step
    For example:
        A tetrachord is 4 notes separated by 2 whole steps then 1 half step
        The 1st tetrachord is: C   D   E   F
        The 2nd tetrachord is: G   A   B   C
        Put together it is: C   D   E   F   G   A   B   C

				min 2nd			min 2nd	
Here are the 12 Ionian scales:	C	D	E	F	G	A	B	C
(see alternate spelling below)	Db	Eb	F	Gb	Ab	Bb	C	Db
	D	E	F#	G	A	B	C#	D
Half-steps between notes:	Eb	F	G	Ab	Bb	C	D	Eb
2-2-1-2-2-2-1	E	F#	G#	A	B	C#	D#	E
	F	G	A	Bb	C	D	E	F
(see alternate spelling below)	F#	G#	A#	B	C#	D#	E#	F#
	G	A	B	C	D	E	F#	G
	Ab	Bb	C	Db	Eb	F	G	Ab
	A	B	C#	D	E	F#	G#	A
	Bb	C	D	Eb	F	G	A	Bb
(see alternate spelling below)	B	C#	D#	E	F#	G#	A#	B

Alternate spelling for Db Ionian:	C#	D#	E#	F#	G#	A#	B#	C#
Alternate spelling for F# Ionian:	Gb	Ab	Bb	Cb	Db	Eb	F	Gb
Alternate spelling for B Ionian:	Cb	Db	Eb	Fb	Gb	Ab	Bb	Cb

Copyright 2013 by Kevin G. Pace
PaceMusicServices.com

Dorian

2nd mode of Ionian (major)
Parent mode: Major 2nd below 1st scale degree. Or 7th note of Dorian scale.
    Example: D Dorian is the 2nd mode of C Major (See #2 under ways to think about the scale).

Interesting or defining features:
Using only white keys, D Dorian is from D to D
Same as natural minor with a sharped (raised) 6th scale degree
Subtract one flat from a minor key signature with flats to find Dorian key
    Example: D minor has 1 flat. D Dorian has no flats.
Add one sharp to a minor key signature with sharps to find Dorian key
    Example: E minor has 1 sharp (F#). E Dorian has 2 sharps (F# & C#).
Minor 2nds between scale degrees 2 & 3, 6 & 7

Chords that may be used with this scale: (examples in C Dorian)
MInor triad (C-Eb-G)　　　Minor 6 (C-Eb-G-A)　　　Minor 13 (C-Eb-G-Bb-D-F-A)
Minor 7 (C-Eb-G-Bb)　　　Minor 9 (C-Eb-G-Bb-D)　　(Minor 13 includes all notes of Dorian)

Here are two ways to think about the Dorian mode:
1-Compare it to another scale
    For example:

D Natural Minor:	D	E	F	G	A	**Bb**	C	D
D Dorian:	D	E	F	G	A	**B**	C	D

Note the difference on scale degree 6. Dorian has a raised 6th scale degree.

2-Think of the notes of the parent scale and invert it
    For example:

C Major:	C	D	E	F	G	A	B	C	
D Dorian:		D	E	F	G	A	B	C	D

Here are the 12 Dorian scales:

Half-steps between notes:
2-1-2-2-2-1-2

	min 2nd				min 2nd		
C	D	Eb	F	G	A	Bb	C
C#	D#	E	F#	G#	A#	B	C#
D	E	F	G	A	B	C	D
Eb	F	Gb	Ab	Bb	C	Db	Eb
E	F#	G	A	B	C#	D	E
F	G	Ab	Bb	C	D	Eb	F
F#	G#	A	B	C#	D#	E	F#
G	A	Bb	C	D	E	F	G
G#	A#	B	C#	D#	E#	F#	G#
A	B	C	D	E	F#	G	A
Bb	C	Db	Eb	F	G	Ab	Bb
B	C#	D	E	F#	G#	A	B

Copyright 2013 by Kevin G. Pace
PaceMusicServices.com

Phrygian

3rd mode of Ionian (major)
Parent mode: Major 3rd below 1st scale degree. Or 6th note of Phrygian scale.
    For example: E Phrygian is the 3rd mode of C Major.
        (See #2 under ways to think about the scale)

Interesting or defining features:
Using only white keys, E Phrygian is from E to E
Same as natural minor with a flatted (lowered) 2nd scale degree
Add one flat to a minor key signature with flats to find Phrygian key
    Example: G minor has 2 flats (Bb & Eb). G Phrygian has 3 flats (Bb, Eb, & Ab).
Subtract one sharp from a minor key signature with sharps to find Phrygian key
    Example: E minor has one sharp. E Phrygian has no sharps.
Minor 2nds between scale degrees 1 & 2, 5 & 6

Chords that may be used with this scale: (examples in C Phrygian)
Minor 7 (C-Eb-G-Bb)   Minor 7sus4(b9) (C-F-G-Bb-Db)
Major 7b5 chord 1/2 step above the root: (Db-F-Abb-C). In other words, play a C Phrygian Scale starting
    on the note 1/2 step lower than the root of the Db Major 7(b5) chord (C is the 7th of the chord).

Here are two ways to think about the Phrygian mode:
1-Compare it to another scale
    For example:

E Natural Minor:	E	**F#**	G	A	B	C	D	E
E Phrygian:	E	**F**	G	A	B	C	D	E

Note the difference on scale degree 2. Phrygian has a lowered 2nd scale degree.

2-Think of the notes of the parent scale and invert it
    For example:

C Major:	C	D	E	F	G	A	B	C
E Phrygian:	E	F	G	A	B	C	D	E

Here are the 12 Phrygian scales:
Half-steps between notes:
1-2-2-2-1-2-2

	min 2nd			min 2nd		
C	Db	Eb	F	G	Ab	Bb	C
C#	D	E	F#	G#	A	B	C#
D	Eb	F	G	A	Bb	C	D
Eb	Fb	Gb	Ab	Bb	Cb	Db	Eb
E	F	G	A	B	C	D	E
F	Gb	Ab	Bb	C	Db	Eb	F
F#	G	A	B	C#	D	E	F#
G	Ab	Bb	C	D	Eb	F	G
G#	A	B	C#	D#	E	F#	G#
A	Bb	C	D	E	F	G	A
Bb	Cb	Db	Eb	F	Gb	Ab	Bb
B	C	D	E	F#	G	A	B

Copyright 2013 by Kevin G. Pace
PaceMusicServices.com

Lydian

4th mode of Ionian (major)
Parent mode: Perfect 4th below 1st scale degree. Or 5th note of Lydian scale.
    For example: F Lydian is the 4th mode of C Major.
        (See #2 under ways to think about the scale)

Interesting or defining features:
Using only white keys, F Lydian is from F to F
Same as Major with a raised (sharped) 4th scale degree
Subtract one flat from a major key signature with flats to find Lydian key
    Example: F Major has 1 flat. F Lydian has no flats.
Add one sharp to a Major key signature with sharps to find Lydian key
    Example: G Major has 1 sharp (F#). G Lydian has 2 sharps (F# & C#).
Minor 2nds between scale degrees 4 & 5, 7 & 8

Chords that may be used with this scale: (examples in C Lydian)
Major triad (C-E-G)   Major 7 (C-E-G-B)
Major 7 (#11) (C-E-G-B-F#)

Here are two ways to think about the Lydian mode:
1-Compare it to another scale
    For example:

F Major (Ionian)	F	G	A	**Bb**	C	D	E	F
F Lydian	F	G	A	**B**	C	D	E	F

Note the difference on scale degree 4. Lydian has a raised 4th scale degree.

2-Think of the notes of the parent scale and invert it
    For example:

C Major:	C	D	E	F	G	A	B	C
F Lydian	F	G	A	B	C	D	E	F

Here are the 12 Lydian scales:

Half-steps between notes:
2-2-2-1-2-2-1

			min 2nd			min 2nd	
C	D	E	F#	G	A	B	C
Db	Eb	F	G	Ab	Bb	C	Db
D	E	F#	G#	A	B	C#	D
Eb	F	G	A	Bb	C	D	Eb
E	F#	G#	A#	B	C#	D#	E
F	G	A	B	C	D	E	F
F#	G#	A#	B#	C#	D#	E#	F#
G	A	B	C#	D	E	F#	G
Ab	Bb	C	D	Eb	F	G	Ab
A	B	C#	D#	E	F#	G#	A
Bb	C	D	E	F	G	A	Bb
B	C#	D#	E#	F#	G#	A#	B

Copyright 2013 by Kevin G. Pace
PaceMusicServices.com

Mixolydian

5th mode of Ionian (major)
Parent mode: Perfect 5th below 1st scale degree. Or 4th note of Mixolydian scale.
    Example: G Mixolydian is the 5th mode of C Major (See #2 under ways to think about the scale).

Interesting or defining features:
Using only white keys, G Mixolydian is from G to G
Same as Major with a lowered (flatted) 7th scale degree
Add one flat to a major key signature with flats to find Mixolydian key
    Example: F Major has 1 flat. F Mixoydian has 2 flats.
Subtract one sharp from a Major key signature with sharps to find Mixolydian key
    Example: G Major has 1 sharp (F#). G Mixolydian has no sharps.
Minor 2nds between scale degrees 4 & 5, 7 & 8

Chords that may be used with this scale: (examples in C Mixolyian)
Dominant 7 (C-E-G-Bb) Dominant 13 (C-E-G-Bb-D-A)
Dominant 9 (C-E-G-Bb-D) Dominant sus 4 (C-F-G-Bb)

Here are two ways to think about the Mixolydian mode:
1-Compare it to another scale
    For example:

G Major (Ionian)	G	A	B	C	D	E	**F#**	G
G Mixolydian	G	A	B	C	D	E	**F**	G

Note the difference on scale degree 7. Mixolydian has a lowered 7th scale degree.

2-Think of the notes of the parent scale and invert it
    For example:

C Major:	C	D	E	F	G	A	B	C
G Mixolydian	G	A	B	C	D	E	F	G

Here are the 12 Mixolydian scales:

Half-steps between notes: 2-2-1-2-2-1-2

(min 2nd between scale degrees 3-4 and 6-7)

C	D	E	F	G	A	Bb	C
Db	Eb	F	Gb	Ab	Bb	Cb	Db
D	E	F#	G	A	B	C	D
Eb	F	G	Ab	Bb	C	Db	Eb
E	F#	G#	A	B	C#	D	E
F	G	A	Bb	C	D	Eb	F
F#	G#	A#	B	C#	D#	E	F#
G	A	B	C	D	E	F	G
Ab	Bb	C	Db	Eb	F	Gb	Ab
A	B	C#	D	E	F#	G	A
Bb	C	D	Eb	F	G	Ab	Bb
B	C#	D#	E	F#	G#	A	B

Copyright 2013 by Kevin G. Pace
PaceMusicServices.com

Aeolian (Natural Minor)

6th mode of Ionian (major)
Parent mode: Major 6th below 1st scale degree. Or 3rd note of Aeolian scale.
    Example: A Aeolian is the 6th mode of C Major (See #2 under ways to think about the scale).

Interesting or defining features:
Using only white keys, A Aeolian is from A to A
Aeolian is another name for the Natural Minor scale
Aeolian shares the same key signature as the Ionian scale a minor 3rd above
    Example: A Aeolian has no sharps or flats. C Ionian has no sharps or flats.
Minor 2nds between scale degrees 2 & 3, 5 & 6

Chords that may be used with this scale: (examples in C Aeolian)
MInor triad (C-Eb-G)
Minor 7 (C-Eb-G-Bb)
Minor 9 (C-Eb-G-Bb-D)
Minor 11 (C-Eb-G-Bb-D-F)

Here are two ways to think about the Aeolian mode:
1-Think of the key signature of the Major scale a minor 3rd higher
    For example:

C Ionian has no sharps or flats	C	D	E	F	G	A	B	C
A Aeolian has no sharps or flats	A	B	C	D	E	F	G	A

2-Think of the notes of the parent scale and invert it
    For example:

C Major (Ionian):	C	D	E	F	G	A	B	C
A minor (Aeolian):	A	B	C	D	E	F	G	A

Here are the 12 Aeolian scales:

		min 2nd		min 2nd		
C	D	Eb	F	G	Ab	Bb	C
C#	D#	E	F#	G#	A	B	C#
D	E	F	G	A	Bb	C	D
Eb	F	Gb	Ab	Bb	Cb	Db	Eb
E	F#	G	A	B	C	D	E
F	G	Ab	Bb	C	Db	Eb	F
F#	G#	A	B	C#	D	E	F#
G	A	Bb	C	D	Eb	F	G
G#	A#	B	C#	D#	E	F#	G#
A	B	C	D	E	F	G	A
Bb	C	Db	Eb	F	Gb	Ab	Bb
B	C#	D	E	F#	G	A	B

Half-steps between notes:
2-1-2-2-1-2-2

Copyright 2013 by Kevin G. Pace
PaceMusicServices.com

Locrian

7th mode of Ionian (major)
Parent mode: Major 7th below 1st scale degree. Or 2nd note of Locrian scale.
    Example: B Locrian is the 7th mode of C Major (See #2 under ways to think about the scale).

Interesting or defining features:
Using only white keys, B Locrian is from B to B
Same as natural minor with a flatted (lowered) 2nd and 5th scale degrees
Add two flats to a minor key signature with flats to find Locrian key
    Example: D minor has 1 flat (Bb). D Locrian has 3 flats (Bb, Eb, & Ab).
Subtract two sharps from a minor key signature with sharps to find Locrian key
    Example: F# minor has three sharps (F#, C#, G#). F# Locrian has one sharp (F#).
Minor 2nds between scale degrees 1 & 2, 4 & 5

Chords that may be used with this scale: (examples in C Locrian)
Diminished triad (C-Eb-Gb)
Half-diminished 7 (C-Eb-Gb-Bb)
Half-diminished 11 (C-Eb-Gb-Bb-F)

Here are two ways to think about the Locrian mode:
1-Compare it to another scale
    For example:

B Natural Minor:	B	**C#**	D	E	**F#**	G	A	B
B Locrian:	B	**C**	D	E	**F**	G	A	B

Note differences on scale degrees 2 & 5. Locrian has lowered 2nd & 5th scale degrees.

2-Think of the notes of the parent scale and invert it
    For example:

C Major:	C	D	E	F	G	A	B	C
B Locrian:	B	C	D	E	F	G	A	B

Here are the 12 Locrian scales:

Half-steps between notes:
1-2-2-1-2-2-2

	min 2nd			min 2nd			
C	Db	Eb	F	Gb	Ab	Bb	C
C#	D	E	F#	G	A	B	C#
D	Eb	F	G	Ab	Bb	C	D
D#	E	F#	G#	A	B	C#	D#
E	F	G	A	Bb	C	D	E
F	Gb	Ab	Bb	Cb	Db	Eb	F
F#	G	A	B	C	D	E	F#
G	Ab	Bb	C	Db	Eb	F	G
G#	A	B	C#	D	E	F#	G#
A	Bb	C	D	Eb	F	G	A
Bb	Cb	Db	Eb	Fb	Gb	Ab	Bb
B	C	D	E	F	G	A	B

Whole Tones (F G A B)

Church Modes - Chords & Scales

Chords			Modes						
Major Triad	Maj 7	Maj 9	Ionian						
Minor Triad	min 7	min 9	2	Dorian					
Minor Triad	min 7		3	2	Phrygian				
Major Triad	Maj 7	Maj 7 (#11)	4	3	2	Lydian			
Dominant 7	Dominant 9		5	4	3	2	Mixolydian		
Minor Triad	min 7		6	5	4	3	2	Aeolian	
Dim Triad	Half Dim 7		7	6	5	4	3	2	Locrian
Major Triad	Maj 7	Maj 9	--------	7	6	5	4	3	2
Minor Triad	min 7	min 9	----------------		7	6	5	4	3
Minor Triad	min 7		------------------------			7	6	5	4
Major Triad	Maj 7	Maj 7 (#11)	--------------------------------				7	6	5
Dominant 7	Dominant 9		--					7	6
Minor Triad	min 7		--						7

(The numbers above represent the scale degrees of the various modes on which you can build the chords shown in the columns to their left).

Each mode is shown with its main chord(s) to the left of its name.

Other possible chords are listed to left of the numbers. Play the chord with its root on the scale degree of the number to its left.

Example: Let's say you are playing a C Lydian scale (C-D-E-F#-G-A-B-C)

1. Find the Lydian heading in the chart.
2. Look to the far left of this heading. You see that the main chords are Major Triad, Major 7, or Major 9.
3. Directly under the heading of Lydian is the number "2". This represents the 2nd scale degree of Lydian. To the far left of this "2" you see Dominant 7 or 9. Play these chords with their root on the 2nd scale degree of Lydian. In other words, play a D7 chord against a C Lydian scale.
4. Continuing down the column under the heading of Lydian is the number "3", representing scale degree 3 of Lydian. To the far left of this "3" you see minor triad or minor 7. Play either of these chords with their root on the 3rd scale degree of Lydian. In other words, play an Em7 chord with a C Lydian scale.
5. Continue in a similar fashion on each scale degree of the Lydian or any of the other modes.

Example #2: Play the C Phrygian mode (C-Db-Eb-F-G-Ab-Bb-C)

1. Find the Phrygian heading in the chart.
2. Look to the far left of this heading. You see that the main chords are minor Triad or Minor 7.
3. Go down below Phrygian's heading to the number "3". This represents the 3rd scale degree of Phrygian. To the far left of this "3" you see Dominant 7 or 9. Play these chords with their root on the 3rd scale degree of Phrygian. In other words, play a Eb7 chord against a C Phrygian scale.

Copyright 2013 by Kevin G. Pace
PaceMusicServices.com

Pg. 11

Pentatonic Mode 1 (Minor Pentatonic)

A five note scale that corresponds to the 5 black keys on the piano from Eb up to Db.
    For example: Eb Pentatonic Mode 1 is Eb-Gb-Ab-Bb-Db

Interesting or defining features: The intervals are all minor 3rds or major 2nds (3 half steps or 2 half steps). Many melodies use Pentatonic because most succession of notes sound pleasant in Pentatonic. Fingerings are sometimes awkward because thumbs sometimes have to play black keys.

Chords that may be used with this scale: (examples in Eb Pentatonic Mode 1)

Minor 7 (Eb-Gb-Bb-Db)   Major triad starting on the 2nd scale degree (Gb-Bb-Db)
Minor 7 (G#-B-D#-F#) a P5 below the tonic. In other words, play this scale a P5 above chord's root.
Minor 7 (C#-E-G#-B) a M2 below the tonic. In other words, play this scale a M2 above chord's root.
Major 6 chord starting on 2nd scale degree (Gb-Bb-Db-Eb). In other words, play an Eb Pent Mode 1
    scale starting on the 6th of the Gb Major 6 chord (Eb is the 6th of the chord).
Minor 7(add 11) (Eb-Gb-Ab-Bb-Db). Or could be thought of as a suspended 7 chord (Eb-Ab-Bb-Db).
Half-dim 7 chord a M2 above tonic (F-Ab-Cb-Eb). In other words, play this scale a M2 below the chord's root.
Half-dim 7 chord a P4 below tonic (A#-C#-E-G#). In other words, play this scale a P4 above the chord's root.
Half-dim 9 chord a m3 below tonic (C-Eb-Gb-Bb-D). In other words, play this scale a m3 above the chord's root.
    (see pg. 91 for more information)

Here are two ways to think about the 1st Pentatonic scale:

1-Compare it to another scale. For example:

Eb Natural Minor:	Eb	F	Gb	Ab	Bb	Cb	Db	Eb
Eb Pentatonic 1	Eb		Gb	Ab	Bb		Db	Eb

Note that it's built on scale degrees 1, 3, 4, 5, and 7 of the natural minor scale

2-Think of the piano's black keys from Eb up to Db. Use the same intervals from other starting notes.

For example:
Eb Pentatonic 1	Eb	Gb	Ab	Bb	Db	Eb
F Pentatonic 1	F	Ab	Bb	C	Eb	F

Possible Finger Patterns: (see below)

Here are the 12 Pentatonic Mode 1 scales:

	minor 3rd			minor 3rd		
C	Eb	F	G	Bb	C	(Pattern #3)
C#	E	F#	G#	B	C#	(Pattern #2)
D	F	G	A	C	D	(Pattern #1)
Eb	Gb	Ab	Bb	Db	Eb	(Pattern #1)
E	G	A	B	D	E	(Pattern #1)
F	Ab	Bb	C	Eb	F	(Pattern #1)
F#	A	B	C#	E	F#	(Pattern #2)
G	Bb	C	D	F	G	(Pattern #3)
G#	B	C#	D#	F#	G#	(Pattern #2)
A	C	D	E	G	A	(Pattern #1)
Bb	Db	Eb	F	Ab	Bb	(Pattern #3)
B	D	E	F#	A	B	(Pattern #3)
	major 2nd	major 2nd	major 2nd			

Half-steps between notes: 3-2-2-3-2

Copyright 2013 by Kevin G. Pace
    PaceMusicServices.com

Possible RH fingerings:
These 3 finger patterns assume you will play multiple octaves. The 4th or 5th finger could be used at the top of a scale.

1	2	3	1	3	1	(Pattern #1)
3	1	2	3	1	3	(Pattern #2)
1	3	1	2	3	1	(Pattern #3)

Pentatonic Mode 2

A five note scale, also known as Major Pentatonic.
The 2nd mode of Pentatonic corresponds to the 5 black keys on a piano from Gb up to Eb
    For example: Gb Pentatonic Mode 2 is Gb-Ab-Bb-Db-Eb

Interesting or defining features:
The intervals are all minor 3rds or major 2nds.
Many melodies use Pentatonic because most succession of notes sound pleasant in Pentatonic.

Chords that may be used with this scale: (examples in C Pentatonic Mode 2)
Major triad (C-E-G)   Dominant 7 (C-E-G-Bb)   Dominant 9 chord (C-E-G-Bb-D)
Major 6 chord (C-E-G-A)
Dominant 9 chord a P5 above the tonic (G-B-D-F-A). In other words, play this scale a P4 above chord's root.
    See pg. 90 for more information on chords and the Major Pentatonic

[P4=Perfect 4th, P5=Perfect 5th, Tonic=Scale Degree 1]

Here are two ways to think about Pentatonic mode 2:
1-Compare it to another scale. For example:

Gb Major	Gb	Ab	Bb	Cb	Db	Eb	F	Gb
Gb Pentatonic 2	Gb	Ab	Bb		Db	Eb		Gb

Note that it's built on scale degrees 1, 2, 3, 5, and 6 of the Major scale

2-Think of the piano's black keys from Gb up to Eb. Use the same intervals from other starting notes.

Example:						
Gb Pentatonic 2	Gb	Ab	Bb	Db	Eb	Gb
Ab Pentatonic 2	Ab	Bb	C	Eb	F	Ab

Possible Finger Patterns: (see below)

Here are the 12 Pentatonic Mode 2 scales:

Gb	Ab	Bb	Db	Eb	Gb	(Pattern #1)
G	A	B	D	E	G	(Pattern #1)
Ab	Bb	C	Eb	F	Ab	(Pattern #3)
A	B	C#	E	F#	A	(Pattern #1)
Bb	C	D	F	G	Bb	(Pattern #2)
B	C#	D#	F#	G#	B	(Pattern #1)
C	D	E	G	A	C	(Pattern #1)
Db	Eb	F	Ab	Bb	Db	(Pattern #1 or #4)
D	E	F#	A	B	D	(Pattern #1)
Eb	F	G	Bb	C	Eb	(Pattern #2)
E	F#	G#	B	C#	E	(Pattern #1)
F	G	A	C	D	F	(Pattern #1)

Half-steps between notes: 2-2-3-2-3

Copyright 2013 by Kevin G. Pace
PaceMusicServices.com

Possible RH fingerings:
These 4 finger patterns assume you will play multiple octaves. The 4th or 5th finger could be used at the top of a scale.

1	2	3	1	2	1	(Pattern #1)
3	1	2	3	1	3	(Pattern #2)
3	4	1	3	1	3	(Pattern #3)
4	5	1	2	3	4	(Pattern #4)

Pg. 13

Pentatonic Mode 3

A five note scale
The 3rd mode of Pentatonic corresponds to the 5 black keys on a piano from Ab up to Gb
    For example: Ab Pentatonic Mode 3 is Ab-Bb-Db-Eb-Gb

Interesting or defining features:
The intervals are all minor 3rds or major 2nds.
One can play practically any succession of notes in a Pentatonic Mode and they sound pleasant.

Chords that may be used with this scale: (examples in Ab Pentatonic Mode 3)
Dominant 9 sus chord (Ab-Db-Eb-Gb-Bb)
Major 6 chord built on the note a M2 below the tonic (Gb-Bb-Db-Eb). In other words, play a Pent 3 scale
    starting on the note a M2 above the Major 6 chord's root (In this example, Ab is a M2 above Gb6's root).
Minor 7 chord built on the note a P5 above the tonic (Eb-Gb-Bb-Db). In other words, play a Pent 3 scale
    starting on the note a P4 above the Minor 7's root (In this example, Ab is a P4 above Ebm7's root).
Dominant 7sus4 chord built on the note a P4 above the tonic (Db-Gb-Ab-Cb). In other words, play a Pent 3
    scale starting on the note a P5 above the chord's root (In this example, Ab if P5 above chord's root).
    [M2=Major 2nd, P4=Perfect 4th, P5=Perfect 5th, Tonic=Scale Degree 1]

Here are two ways to think about Pentatonic mode 3:
1-Compare it to another scale. For example:

Ab minor	Ab	Bb	Cb	Db	Eb	Fb	Gb	Ab
Ab Pentatonic 3	Ab	Bb		Db	Eb		Gb	Ab

Note that it's built on scale degrees 1, 2, 4, 5, and 7 of the natural minor scale

2-Think of the piano's black keys from Ab up to Gb. Use the same intervals from other starting notes
    For example:

Ab Pentatonic 3	Ab	Bb	Db	Eb	Gb	Ab
Bb Pentatonic 3	Bb	C	Eb	F	Ab	Bb

Here are the 12 Pentatonic Mode 3 scales:

Half-steps between notes: 2-3-2-3-2

Possible Finger Patterns: (see below)

major 2nd	major 2nd		major 2nd		
Ab	Bb	Db	Eb	Gb	Ab	(Pattern #1)
A	B	D	E	G	A	(Pattern #1)
Bb	C	Eb	F	Ab	Bb	(Pattern #2)
B	C#	E	F#	A	B	(Pattern #3)
C	D	F	G	Bb	C	(Pattern #1)
C#	D#	F#	G#	B	C#	(Pattern #1)
D	E	G	A	C	D	(Pattern #1)
Eb	F	Ab	Bb	Db	Eb	(Pattern #2)
E	F#	A	B	D	E	(Pattern #1)
F	G	Bb	C	Eb	F	(Pattern #1)
F#	G#	B	C#	E	F#	(Pattern #3)
G	A	C	D	F	G	(Pattern #2)

            minor 3rd   minor 3rd

Copyright 2013 by Kevin G. Pace
PaceMusicServices.com

Possible RH fingerings:
These 3 finger patterns assume you will play multiple octaves. The 4th or 5th finger could be used at the top of a scale.

1	2	3	1	2	1	(Pattern #1)
3	1	2	3	1	3	(Pattern #2)
3	4	1	3	1	3	(Pattern #3)

Pentatonic Mode 4

A five note scale
The 4th mode of Pentatonic corresponds to the 5 black keys on a piano from Bb up to Ab
    For example: Bb Pentatonic Mode 4 is Bb-Db-Eb-Gb-Ab

Interesting or defining features:
The intervals are all minor 3rds or major 2nds.
One can play practically any succession of notes in a Pentatonic Mode and they sound pleasant.

Chords that may be used with this scale: (examples in Bb Pentatonic Mode 4)
Minor 7(#5) (Bb-Db-Gb-Ab). This is the same as Gb(add 9) in 2nd inversion.
Major 6 chord built on the note a M3 below the tonic (Gb-Bb-Db-Eb). In other words, play a Pent 4 Scale
    starting on the note a M3 above the Major 6's root (In this example, Bb is a M3 above the chord's root).
Minor 7 chord built on the note a P4 up from the tonic (Eb-Gb-Bb-Db). In other words, play a Pent 4 Scale
    starting on the note a P5 above the chord's root (In this example, Bb is a P5 above the chord's root).
Dominant 7sus chord built on the note a M2 below the tonic (Ab-Db-Eb-Gb). In other words, play a Pent 4 Scale
    starting on the note a M2 above the chord's root (In this example, Bb is a M2 above the chord's root).
    [M2=Major 2nd, M3=Major 3rd, P4=Perfect 4th, P5=Perfect 5th, Tonic=Scale Degree #1]

Here are two ways to think about Pentatonic mode 4:
1-Compare it to another scale. For example:

Bb minor	Bb	Cb	Db	Eb	Fb	Gb	Ab	Bb
Ab Pentatonic 3	Bb		Db	Eb		Gb	Ab	Bb

Note that it's built on scale degrees 1, 3, 4, 6, and 7 of the natural minor scale

2-Think of the piano's black keys from Bb up to Ab. Use the same intervals from other starting notes.

For example: Bb Pentatonic 4	Bb	Db	Eb	Gb	Ab	Bb
C Pentatonic 4	C	Eb	F	Ab	Bb	C

Here are the 12 Pentatonic Mode 4 scales:

Half-steps between notes: 3-2-3-2-2

					Possible Finger Patterns: (see below)
Bb	Db	Eb	Gb	Ab	Bb	(Pattern #1)
B	D	E	G	A	B	(Pattern #1)
C	Eb	F	Ab	Bb	C	(Pattern #3)
C#	E	F#	A	B	C#	(Pattern #2)
D	F	G	Bb	C	D	(Pattern #2)
D#	F#	G#	B	C#	D#	(Pattern #1)
E	G	A	C	D	E	(Pattern #1)
F	Ab	Bb	Db	Eb	F	(Pattern #1)
F#	A	B	D	E	F#	(Pattern #2)
G	Bb	C	Eb	F	G	(Pattern #3)
G#	B	C#	E	F#	G#	(Pattern #4)
A	C	D	F	G	A	(Pattern #1)

Copyright 2013 by Kevin G. Pace
PaceMusicServices.com

Possible RH fingerings:
These 4 finger patterns assume you will play multiple octaves. The 4th or 5th finger could be used at the top of some scales.

1	2	3	1	2	1	(Pattern #1)
3	1	2	3	1	3	(Pattern #2)
1	3	1	2	3	1	(Pattern #3)
3	1	3	1	2	3	(Pattern #4)

Pentatonic Mode 5

A five note scale
The 5th mode of Pentatonic corresponds to the 5 black keys on a piano from Db up to Bb
    For example: Bb Pentatonic Mode 5 is Db-Eb-Gb-Ab-Bb

Interesting or defining features: The intervals are all minor 3rds or major 2nds.
One can play practically any succession of notes in a Pentatonic Mode and they sound pleasant.

Chords that may be used with this scale: (examples in Db Pentatonic Mode 5)
sus chord (Db-Gb-Ab)
Major 6 chord built on the note a P4 up from the tonic (Gb-Bb-Db-Eb). In other words, play a Pent 5
    scale starting on the note a P5 up from the chord's root (in this example, Db is a P5 above Gb6's root).
Minor 7 chord built on the note a M2 above the tonic (Eb-Gb-Bb-Db). In other words, play a Pent 5 scale
    on the note a M2 below the chord's root (in this example, Db is a M2 above chord's root).
Dominant 7 sus chord built on the note a P5 up from the tonic (Ab-Db-Eb-Gb). In other words, Play a Pent 5
    scale starting on note a P4 above the chord's root (in this example, Db is a P4 above the chord's root).

Here are two ways to think about Pentatonic mode 5:
1-Compare it to another scale. For example:

Db Major	Db	Eb	F	Gb	Ab	Bb	C	Db
Db Pentatoic 5	Db	Eb		Gb	Ab	Bb		Db

Note that it's built on scale degrees 1, 2, 4, 5, and 6 of the Major scale

2-Think of the piano's black keys from Bb up to Ab. Use the same intervals from other starting notes.
For example: Db Pentatonic 5   Db Eb Gb Ab Bb Db
             E Pentatonic 5   E F# A B C# E

Here are the 12 Pentatonic Mode 5 scales:

Possible Finger Patterns: (see below)

Db	Eb	Gb	Ab	Bb	Db	(Pattern #1)
D	E	G	A	B	D	(Pattern #1)
Eb	F	Ab	Bb	C	Eb	(Pattern #2)
E	F#	A	B	C#	E	(Pattern #1)
F	G	Bb	C	D	F	(Pattern #1)
F#	G#	B	C#	D#	F#	(Pattern #1)
G	A	C	D	E	G	(Pattern #1)
Ab	Bb	Db	Eb	F	Ab	(Pattern #4)
A	B	D	E	F#	A	(Pattern #1)
Bb	C	Eb	F	G	Bb	(Pattern #2)
B	C#	E	F#	G#	B	(Pattern #3)
C	D	F	G	A	C	(Pattern #1)

Half-steps between notes: 2-3-2-2-3

Copyright 2013 by Kevin G. Pace
    PaceMusicServices.com

Possible RH fingerings:
These 4 finger patterns assume you will play multiple octaves. The 4th or 5th finger could be used at the top of some scales.

1	2	3	1	2	1	(Pattern #1)
3	1	2	3	1	3	(Pattern #2)
1	3	1	2	3	1	(Pattern #3)
3	4	1	3	1	3	(Pattern #4)

Pg. 16

Bebop 7th or Bebop Dominant Scale

A Major scale with an added b7, making it an eight note scale.

Interesting or defining features:
Minor 2nds between scale degrees 3 & 4, 6 & 7, 7 & 8, 8 & 1

Chords that may be used with this scale: (examples in C Bebop 7)
Dominant 7 (C-E-G-Bb)   Dominant 9 (C-E-G-Bb-D)
Minor 7 built on 5th scale degree (G-Bb-D-F). In other words, play a Bebop 7th scale on the note a P4 above the chord's root. (In this example, C is a P4 above the G minor7's root).

Here are two ways to think about the Bebop 7 scale:
1-Think of its intervals
    For example: W   W   H   W   W   H   H   H
        W=Whole step or 2 half steps   H=Half step

2-Play a major scale with an added b7 between scale degrees 6 & 7
For example: C Major: C   D   E   F   G   A   B   C
             C Bebop 7:   C   D   E   F   G   A   Bb   B   C

Here are the 12 Bebop 7 scales with possible right hand fingerings:

(see alternate spelling below)

Half-steps between notes:
    2-2-1-2-2-1-1-1

(see alternate spelling below)

Copyright 2013 by Kevin G. Pace
PaceMusicServices.com

		min 2nd			min 2nd		
						min 2nd	
							min 2nd
2 C	3 D	4 E	1 F	2 G	3 A	4 Bb	1 B	2 C
3 Db	4 Eb	1 F	2 Gb	3 Ab	4 Bb	1 Cb	2 C	3 Db
1 D	2 E	3 F#	4 G	1 A	2 B	3 C	4 C#	1 D
3 Eb	1 F	2 G	3 Ab	4 Bb	1 C	3 Db	1 D	3 Eb
1 E	2 F#	3 G#	1 A	2 B	3 C#	1 D	3 D#	1 E
1 F	2 G	3 A	4 Bb	1 C	2 D	3 Eb	4 E	1 F
2 F#	3 G#	4 A#	1 B	2 C#	3 D#	4 E	1 E#	2 F#
1 G	2 A	3 B	4 C	1 D	2 E	3 F	4 F#	1 G
3 Ab	4 Bb	1 C	2 Db	3 Eb	1 F	3 Gb	1 G	3 Ab
1 A	2 B	3 C#	4 D	1 E	2 F#	3 G	4 G#	1 A
3 Bb	1 C	2 D	3 Eb	1 F	2 G	3 Ab	1 A	3 Bb
1 B	2 C#	3 D#	1 E	2 F#	3 G#	1 A	3 A#	1 B

Alternate spelling for Db Bebop 7:   C#   D#   E#   F#   G#   A#   B   B#   C#
Alternate spelling for F# Bebop 7:   Gb   Ab   Bb   Cb   Db   Eb   Fb   F   Gb

Pg. 17
Bebop Major Scale

A Major scale with an added b6, making it an eight note scale.

Interesting or defining features:
Minor 2nds between scale degrees 3 & 4, 5 & 6, 6 & 7, 8 & 1

Chords that may be used with this scale: (examples in C Major)
Major 6 (C-E-G-A)
Major 7 (C-E-G-B)

Here are two ways to think about the Bebop Major scale:
1-Think of its intervals
   For example:

   W W H W H H W H
   W=Whole step or 2 half steps   H=Half step

2-Play a major scale with an added b6 between scale degrees 5 & 6
   For example:
   C Major: C   D   E   F   G   A   B   C
   C Bebop Major: C   D   E   F   G   Ab   A   B   C

Here are the 12 Bebop Major scales with possible RH fingerings:

(see alternate spelling below)

Half-steps between notes:
2-2-1-2-1-1-2-1

			min 2nd	min 2nd		min 2nd	
1	2	3	1	2	3	1	2	1

1 C	2 D	3 E	1 F	2 G	3 Ab	1 A	2 B	1 C
2 Db	3 Eb	1 F	2 Gb	3 Ab	1 Bbb	2 Bb	1 C	2 Db
1 D	2 E	3 F#	1 G	2 A	3 Bb	1 B	2 C#	1 D
4 Eb	1 F	2 G	3 Ab	4 Bb	1 Cb	2 C	3 D	4 Eb
1 E	2 F#	3 G#	1 A	2 B	1 C	2 C#	3 D#	1 E
1 F	2 G	3 A	4 Bb	1 C	2 Db	3 D	4 E	1 F
2 F#	3 G#	4 A#	1 B	2 C#	1 D	2 D#	1 E#	2 F#
1 G	2 A	3 B	1 C	2 D	3 Eb	1 E	2 F#	1 G
2 Ab	3 Bb	1 C	2 Db	3 Eb	1 Fb	2 F	1 G	2 Ab
1 A	2 B	3 C#	4 D	1 E	2 F	3 F#	4 G#	1 A
3 Bb	1 C	2 D	3 Eb	1 F	2 Gb	1 G	2 A	3 Bb
1 B	2 C#	3 D#	1 E	2 F#	1 G	2 G#	3 A#	1 B

Copyright 2013 by Kevin G. Pace
PaceMusicServices.com

Alternate spelling of Db Bebop Major:
C#   D#   E#   F#   G#   A   A#   C   C#

Blues Minor Scale

A six note scale. Like the Pentatonic Mode 1 with an added #4 or b5.

Interesting or defining features:
Minor 3rd, whole step, half step, half step, minor 3rd, whole step

Chords that may be used with this scale: (examples in C Blues minor)
Dominant 7 built on scale degree 1 (C-E-G-Bb)   Dominant 7 built on scale degree 4 (F-A-C-Eb)
Dominant 7 built on scale degree 5 (G-B-D-F)   Minor 7 (C-Eb-G-Bb)

Here are two ways to think about the Blues Minor scale:
1-Think of its intervals: m3   W   H   H   m3   W
    W=Whole step or 2 half steps   H=Half step   m3=minor 3rd or 3 half steps

2-Play a pentatonic mode 1 scale with an added #4 or b5. For example:
    C Pentatonic Mode 1:   C   Eb   F   G   Bb   C
    C minor blues scale: C   Eb   F   F#   G   Bb   C

Here are the 12 Blues Minor scales with possible right hand fingering:
(Note: the last finger number is assuming you will continue on to another octave. If only playing one octave you could substitute another finger number.)

Half-steps between notes:

    3-2-1-1-3-2

1	2	3	4	1	2	1	Alternate fingering
C	Eb	F	F#	G	Bb	C	1-3-1-3-1-3-1
2	3	4	1	2	1	2	3-1-3-1-3-1-3
Db	Fb	Gb	G	Ab	Cb	Db	
1	2	3	4	1	2	1	
D	F	G	G#	A	C	D	
1	2	3	1	2	3	1	
Eb	Gb	Ab	A	Bb	Db	Eb	
1	2	3	4	1	2	1	
E	G	A	A#	B	D	E	
1	2	3	1	2	3	1	
F	Ab	Bb	B	C	Eb	F	
2	1	2	3	4	1	2	2-3-1-2-3-1-2
F#	A	B	B#	C#	E	F#	
3	4	1	2	1	2	3	1-3-1-3-1-2-1
G	Bb	C	C#	D	F	G	
4	1	2	1	2	3	4	4-1-3-1-2-3-4
Ab	Cb	Db	D	Eb	Gb	Ab	
1	2	3	4	1	2	1	
A	C	D	D#	E	G	A	
1	2	3	1	2	3	1	
Bb	Db	Eb	E	F	Ab	Bb	
1	2	3	1	2	3	1	
B	D	E	E#	F#	A	B	

min 2nd appears between columns 3-4 and 4-5; min 3rd appears between columns 1-2 and 5-6.

Copyright 2013 by Kevin G. Pace
PaceMusicServices.com

Pg. 19

Blues Major Scale

1st Inversion of blues minor scale.   Like the Pentatonic Mode 2 with an added #2 or b3.
A six note scale.

Interesting or defining features: Whole step, half step, half step, minor 3rd, whole step, minor 3rd

Chords that may be used with this scale: (examples in C Blues Major)

Dominant 7 built on scale degree 1 (C-E-G-Bb)   Major 7 built on scale degree 1 (C-E-G-B)
Dominant 9 built on scale degree 1 (C-E-G-Bb-D)   Major 9 built on scale degree 1 (C-E-G-B-D)
Minor 6 (C-Eb-G-A)   Major 6 (C-E-G-A)
Dominant 13 (no 11) built on scale degree 1 (C-E-G-Bb-D-A)

Here are two ways to think about the Blues Major scale:
1-Think of its intervals   W   H   H   m3   W   m3
          W=Whole step or 2 half steps   H=Half step   m3=minor 3rd or 3 half steps

2-Play a pentatonic mode 2 scale with an added #2 or b3. For example:
          C Pentatonic Mode 2:   C   D   E   G   A   C
          C Major Blues scale: C   D   D#   E   G   A   C

Here are the 12 Blues Major scales with possible right hand fingerings:

Half-steps between notes:
          2-1-1-3-2-3

Alternate fingerings

3-1-3-1-3-1-3

		min 2nd			
	min 2nd				
1	2	3	1	2	3	1
C	D	D#	E	G	A	C
2	3	1	2	3	1	2
Db	Eb	E	F	Ab	Bb	Db
2	3	1	2	3	1	2
D	E	F	Gb	A	B	D
2	3	4	1	2	1	2
Eb	F	F#	G	Bb	C	Eb
3	4	1	2	1	2	3
E	F#	G	Ab	B	C#	E
1	2	3	1	2	3	1
F	G	G#	A	C	D	F
2	3	1	2	3	1	2
Gb	Ab	A	Bb	Db	Eb	Gb
2	3	4	1	2	1	2
G	A	A#	B	D	E	G
2	3	1	2	3	1	2
Ab	Bb	B	C	Eb	F	Ab
1	2	3	4	1	2	1
A	B	C	Db	E	F#	A
4	1	2	1	2	3	4
Bb	C	C#	D	F	G	Bb
1	3	1	2	3	4	1
B	C#	D	D#	F#	G#	B
		min 3rd		min 3rd		

Copyright 2013 by Kevin G. Pace
PaceMusicServices.com

Whole Tone Scale

This scale is composed of only whole steps
A six note scale

Interesting or defining features:
All whole steps

Chords that may be used with this scale: (examples in C)
Augmented triad (C-E-G#)
Augmented 7 chord (C-E-G#-Bb). This chord is also called dominant 7(#5).
Augmented 9(#11) (C-E-G#-Bb-D-F#). Augmented 9(#11) includes all notes from the whole tone scale.

Here are two ways to think about the Whole Tone scale:
1-Think of its intervals
    For example:

                W   W   W   W   W

    W=Whole step or 2 half steps

2-Think about white key & black key patterns
    For example:

C Whole Tone scale:	C	D	E	F#	G#	A#	C
Db Whole Tone scale:	Db	Eb	F	G	A	B	Db

Note that if you play the 3 black keys, you will play the 3 white keys surrounding the 2 black keys.
Note that if you play the 2 black keys, you will play the 4 white keys surrounding the 3 black keys.

Here are the 12 Whole Tone scales:

	C	D	E	F#	G#	A#	C
	Db	Eb	F	G	A	B	Db
	D	E	F#	G#	A#	C	D
Half-steps between notes:	Eb	F	G	A	B	Db	Eb
2-2-2-2-2	E	F#	G#	A#	C	D	E
	F	G	A	B	Db	Eb	F
	Gb	Ab	Bb	C	D	E	Gb
	G	A	B	Db	Eb	F	G
	Ab	Bb	C	D	E	Gb	Ab
	A	B	C#	D#	F	G	A
	Bb	C	D	E	Gb	Ab	Bb
	B	C#	D#	F	G	A	B

Copyright 2013 by Kevin G. Pace
    PaceMusicServices.com

Fingering guidelines: Keep your thumb off the black keys.

Melodic Minor Scale

Melodic Minor is the parent scale of several modes, covered in the next pages.
It could also be thought of as Dorian #7 or Ionian b3.
It is an Aeolian scale with a sharped 6 & 7 scale degree.
> Example: A Melodic Minor is the same as A Aeolian, but with F# & G#
> (See below under ways to think about the scale).

Interesting or defining features:
The bottom half of this scale is minor. The top half is Major.
Minor 2nds between scale degrees 2 & 3, 7 & 8

Chords that may be used with this scale: (examples in C Melodic Minor)
Minor triad (C-Eb-G)
Minor-Major 7 (C-Eb-G-B)
Minor-Major 9 (C-Eb-G-B-D)

Here are three ways to think about the Melodic Minor scale:
1-Compare it to other scales
For example:

C Ionian:	C	D	E	F	G	A	B	C
C Melodic Minor:	C	D	Eb	F	G	A	B	C

or

C Dorian:	C	D	Eb	F	G	A	Bb	C
C Melodic Minor:	C	D	Eb	F	G	A	B	C

or

C Aeolian:	C	D	Eb	F	G	Ab	Bb	C
C Melodic Minor:	C	D	Eb	F	G	A	B	C

Here are the 12 Melodic Minor scales:

(min 2nd between scale degrees 2 & 3, and 7 & 8)

Half-steps between notes: 2-1-2-2-2-2-1

C	D	Eb	F	G	A	B	C
Db	Eb	Fb	Gb	Ab	Bb	C	Db
D	E	F	G	A	B	C#	D
Eb	F	Gb	Ab	Bb	C	D	Eb
E	F#	G	A	B	C#	D#	E
F	G	Ab	Bb	C	D	E	F
F#	G#	A	B	C#	D#	E#	F#
G	A	Bb	C	D	E	F#	G
Ab	Bb	Cb	Db	Eb	F	G	Ab
A	B	C	D	E	F#	G#	A
Bb	C	Db	Eb	F	G	A	Bb
B	C#	D	E	F#	G#	A#	B

Copyright 2013 by Kevin G. Pace
PaceMusicServices.com

Phrygian #6

2nd mode of Melodic Minor. Also called Dorian b2.
Parent mode: Major 2nd below 1st scale degree. Or 7th note of Phrygian #6 scale.
    For example: D Phrygian #6 is the 2nd mode of C Melodic Minor.
        (See #2 under ways to think about the scale)

Interesting or defining features:
Minor 2nds between scale degrees 1 & 2, 6 & 7

Chords that may be used with this scale: (examples in C Phrygian #6)
Minor 7 (C-Eb-G-Bb)
Minor-Major 7 of 7th degree of scale (Bb-Db-F-A). In other words, play a Phrygian #6 scale starting
    on the note a M2 above this chord's root (in this example, C is a M2 above the chord's root).
Minor 6 (C-Eb-G-A)

Here are two ways to think about the Phrygian #6 scale:
1-Compare it to other scales
    For example:

E Natural Minor:	E	**F#**	G	A	B	C	D	E
E Phrygian:	E	**F**	G	A	B	**C**	D	E
E Phrygian #6:	E	F	G	A	B	**C#**	D	E

Note the differences all occur on scale degrees 2 & 6. Why?
Phrygian is Natural Minor with a flatted (lowered) 2nd scale degree
Phrygian #6 is, as the name implies, a Phrygian scale with a sharped (raised) 6th scale degree

2-Think of the notes of the parent scale and invert it
    For example:

D Melodic Minor:	D	E	F	G	A	B	C#	D
E Phrygian #6:	E	F	G	A	B	C#	D	E

Here are the 12 Phrygian #6 scales

Half-steps between notes:
1-2-2-2-2-1-2

C	Db	Eb	F	G	A	Bb	C
C#	D	E	F#	G#	A#	B	C#
D	Eb	F	G	A	B	C	D
D#	E	F#	G#	A#	B#	C#	D#
E	F	G	A	B	C#	D	E
F	Gb	Ab	Bb	C	D	Eb	F
F#	G	A	B	C#	D#	E	F#
G	Ab	Bb	C	D	E	F	G
G#	A	B	C#	D#	E#	F#	G#
A	Bb	C	D	E	F#	G	A
A#	B	C#	D#	E#	Fx	G#	A#
B	C	D	E	F#	G#	A	B

min 2nd (between degrees 1 & 2), min 2nd (between degrees 6 & 7)

Lydian Augmented Scale

3rd mode of Melodic Minor
Parent mode: minor 3rd below 1st scale degree. Or 6th note of the Lydian Augmented scale.
    For example: Eb Lydian Augmented is the 3rd mode of C Melodic Minor.
      (See #2 under ways to think about the scale)

Interesting or defining features:
Minor 2nds between scale degrees 5 & 6, 7 & 8

Chords that may be used with this scale: (examples in C Lydian Augmented)
Augmented Major 7 (C-E-G#-B)

Aug Major 13(#11) (C-E-G#-B-D-F#-A). Or think this way:

$$\frac{\text{D Major Triad}}{\text{C Aug Maj 7}} \quad \left[\frac{\text{Major Triad M2 above root}}{\text{Root Aug Major 7}}\right]$$

Here are two ways to think about the Lydian Augmented scale:

1-Compare it to other scales
    For example:

F Major:	F	G	A	**Bb**	C	D	E	F
F Lydian:	F	G	A	**B**	**C**	D	E	F
F Lydian Augmented:	F	G	A	B	**C#**	D	E	F

    Note the differences all occur on scale degrees 4 & 5. Why?
    Lydian is Major with a sharped (raised) 4th scale degree
    Lydian Augmented is a Lydian scale with a sharped (raised) 5th scale degree

2-Think of the notes of the parent scale and invert it
    For example:

C Melodic Minor:	C	D	Eb	F	G	A	B	C
Eb Lydian Aug:	Eb	F	G	A	B	C	D	Eb

Here are the 12 Lydian Aug scales:

Half-steps between notes:
2-2-2-2-1-2-1

		whole tones				
C	D	E	F#	G#	A	B	C
Db	Eb	F	G	A	Bb	C	Db
D	E	F#	G#	A#	B	C#	D
Eb	F	G	A	B	C	D	Eb
E	F#	G#	A#	B#	C#	D#	E
F	G	A	B	C#	D	E	F
Gb	Ab	Bb	C	D	Eb	F	Gb
G	A	B	C#	D#	E	F#	G
Ab	Bb	C	D	E	F	G	Ab
A	B	C#	D#	E#	F#	G#	A
Bb	C	D	E	F#	G	A	Bb
B	C#	D#	E#	Fx	G#	A#	B

                                              min 2nd   min 2nd

Copyright 2013 by Kevin G. Pace
PaceMusicServices.com

Lydian Dominant Scale

4th mode of Melodic Minor
Could also be called Mixolydian #4 or Lydian b7. Also known as the overtone scale.
Parent mode: Perfect 4th below 1st scale degree. Or 5th note of the Lydian Dominant scale.
    For example: F Lydian Dominant is the 4th mode of C Melodic Minor.
        (See #2 under ways to think about the scale)

Interesting or defining features:
Minor 2nds between scale degrees 4 & 5, 6 & 7

Chords that may be used with this scale: (examples in C Lydian Dominant)
Dominant 7 (C-E-G-Bb)　　　　Major 6 (C-E-G-A)　　　Dominant 7(b5) (C-E-Gb-Bb)
Dominant 13(#11) (C-E-G-Bb-D-F#-A). Or think this way:　　[D Major Triad]　　[Major Triad M2 above root]
(Dominant 13(#11) includes all notes from Lydian Dominant)　[C Dominant 7]　　　[Root Dom 7]

Here are two ways to think about the Lydian Dominant scale:
1-Compare it to other scales
    For example:

G Major:	G	A	B	C	D	E	**F#**	G
G Mixolydian:	G	A	B	**C**	D	E	**F**	G
G Lydian Dominant:	G	A	B	**C#**	D	E	F	G

    Note the differences all occur on scale degrees 4 & 7. Why?
    Mixolydian is Major with a flatted (lowered) 7th scale degree
    Lydian Dominant is a Mixolydian scale with a sharped (raised) 4th scale degree

2-Think of the notes of the parent scale and invert it
    For example:

C Melodic Minor:	C	D	Eb	F	G	A	B	C
F Lydian Dominant:	F	G	A	B	C	D	Eb	F

Here are the 12 Lydian Dominant scales:

Half-steps between notes:
2-2-2-1-2-1-2

C	D	E	F#	G	A	Bb	C
Db	Eb	F	G	Ab	Bb	Cb	Db
D	E	F#	G#	A	B	C	D
Eb	F	G	A	Bb	C	Db	Eb
E	F#	G#	A#	B	C#	D	E
F	G	A	B	C	D	Eb	F
F#	G#	A#	B#	C#	D#	E	F#
G	A	B	C#	D	E	F	G
Ab	Bb	C	D	Eb	F	Gb	Ab
A	B	C#	D#	E	F#	G	A
Bb	C	D	E	F	G	Ab	Bb
B	C#	D#	E#	F#	G#	A	B

                              [min 2nd] [min 2nd]

Copyright 2013 by Kevin G. Pace
PaceMusicServices.com

Mixolydian b6 Scale

5th mode of Melodic Minor
Could also be called Aeolian #3, Mixolydian b13, or Hindu.
Parent mode: Perfect 5th below 1st scale degree. Or 4th note of the Mixolydian b6 scale.
    For example: G Mixolydian b6 is the 5th mode of C Melodic Minor.
        (See #2 under ways to think about the scale)

Interesting or defining features:
Minor 2nds between scale degrees 3 & 4, 5 & 6

Chords that may be used with this scale: (examples in C Mixolydian b6)
Dominant 7 (C-E-G-Bb)   Dominant 7(#5) (C-E-G#-Bb)
Dominant 7 sus (C-F-G-Bb)

Here are two ways to think about the Mixolydian b6 scale:
1-Compare it to other scales
    For example:

A Major:	A	B	C#	D	E	F#	**G#**	A
A Mixolydian:	A	B	C#	D	E	**F#**	**G**	A
A Mixolydian b6:	A	B	C#	D	E	**F**	G	A

Note the differences all occur on scale degrees 6 & 7. Why?
Mixolydian is Major with a flatted (lowered) 7th scale degree
Mixolydian b6 is a Mixolydian scale with a flatted (lowered) 6th scale degree

2-Think of the notes of the parent scale and invert it
    For example:

C Melodic Minor:	C	D	Eb	F	G	A	B	C
G Mixolydian b6	G	A	B	C	D	Eb	F	G

Here are the 12 Mixolyd b6 scales:

C	D	E	F	G	Ab	Bb	C
C#	D#	E#	F#	G#	A	B	C#
D	E	F#	G	A	Bb	C	D
Eb	F	G	Ab	Bb	Cb	Db	Eb
E	F#	G#	A	B	C	D	E
F	G	A	Bb	C	Db	Eb	F
F#	G#	A#	B	C#	D	E	F#
G	A	B	C	D	Eb	F	G
Ab	Bb	C	Db	Eb	Fb	Gb	Ab
A	B	C#	D	E	F	G	A
Bb	C	D	Eb	F	Gb	Ab	Bb
B	C#	D#	E	F#	G	A	B

Half-steps between notes:
2-2-1-2-1-2-2

min 2nd between scale degrees 3 & 4, and 5 & 6

Locrian #2 Scale

6th mode of Melodic Minor
Could also be thought of as Aeolian (Natural Minor) b5.
Parent mode: Major 6th below 1st scale degree. Or 3rd note of the Locrian #2 scale.
    For example: A Locrian #2 is the 6th mode of C Melodic Minor.
      (See #2 under ways to think about the scale)

Interesting or defining features:
Minor 2nds between scale degrees 2 & 3, 4 & 5

Chords that may be used with this scale: (examples in C Locrian #2)
Half-diminished (C-Eb-Gb-Bb). This is also called Minor7(b5).

Here are two ways to think about the Locrian #2 scale:
1-Compare it to other scales
    For example:

B minor:	B	**C#**	D	E	**F#**	G	A	B
B Locrian:	B	**C**	D	E	**F**	G	A	B
A Locrian #2:	B	**C#**	D	E	**F**	G	A	B

Note the differences all occur on scale degrees 2 & 5. Why?
Locrian is minor with a flatted (lowered) 2nd & 5th scale degree
Locrian #2 is a Locrian scale with a sharped (raised) 2nd scale degree

2-Think of the notes of the parent scale and invert it
    For example:

C Melodic Minor:	C	D	Eb	F	G	A	B	C
A Locrian #2	A	B	C	D	Eb	F	G	A

Here are the 12 Locrian #2 scales:

Half-steps between notes:
2-1-2-1-2-2-2

C	D	Eb	F	Gb	Ab	Bb	C
C#	D#	E	F#	G	A	B	C#
D	E	F	G	Ab	Bb	C	D
D#	E#	F#	G#	A	B	C#	D#
E	F#	G	A	Bb	C	D	E
F	G	Ab	Bb	Cb	Db	Eb	F
F#	G#	A	B	C	D	E	F#
G	A	Bb	C	Db	Eb	F	G
G#	A#	B	C#	D	E	F#	G#
A	B	C	D	Eb	F	G	A
Bb	C	Db	Eb	Fb	Gb	Ab	Bb
B	C#	D	E	F	G	A	B

min 2nd   min 2nd

Pg. 27

Altered Scale

7th mode of Melodic Minor. Also called Super Locrian or Locrian b4.
Could also be thought of as Ionian (Major) 1, b2, #2, 3, b5, #5, b7
Parent mode: Major 7th below 1st scale degree. Or 2nd note of the Altered scale.
    For example: B Altered is the 7th mode of C Melodic Minor.
        (See #2 under ways to think about the scale)

Interesting or defining features: Minor 2nds between scale degrees 1 & 2, 3 & 4

Chords that may be used with this scale: (examples in C Altered)
Dominant 7 (C-E-G-Bb)
Altered Dominant 7. (Dominant 7 with any combination of b5, #5, b9, and/or #9).
    For example: C7(#5) = C-E-G#-Bb or C7(b9/b5) = C-E-Gb-Bb-Db.
Minor 7(b5) (C-Eb-Gb-Bb). (This is also called half-diminished).

Here are three ways to think about the Altered scale:
1-Compare it to other scales. For example:

B minor:	B	**C#**	D	E	**F#**	G	A	B
B Locrian:	B	**C**	D	**E**	**F**	G	A	B
B Altered:	B	**C**	D	**Eb**	F	G	A	B

Note the differences all occur on scale degrees 2, 4, & 5. Why?
Locrian is minor with a flatted (lowered) 2nd & 5th scale degree.
Altered is a Locrian scale with a flatted (lowered) 4th scale degree.

2-Think of the notes of the parent scale and invert it
    For example:

C Melodic Minor:	C	D	Eb	F	G	A	B	C
B Altered	B	C	D	Eb	F	G	A	B

		(b9)	(#9)					
3-Major scale with the following scale degrees:	1	b2	#2	3	b5	#5	b7	1
C Altered:	C	Db	D#	E	Gb	G#	Bb	C

Here are the 12 Altered scales: [Scale degrees 4 to 8 are all whole tones]

Half-steps between notes:
    1-2-1-2-2-2-2

C	Db	Eb	Fb	Gb	Ab	Bb	C
C#	D	E	F	G	A	B	C#
D	Eb	F	Gb	Ab	Bb	C	D
D#	E	F#	G	A	B	C#	D#
E	F	G	Ab	Bb	C	D	E
E#	F#	G#	A	B	C#	D#	E#
F#	G	A	Bb	C	D	E	F#
G	Ab	Bb	Cb	Db	Eb	F	G
G#	A	B	C	D	E	F#	G#
A	Bb	C	Db	Eb	F	G	A
A#	B	C#	D	E	F#	G#	A#
B	C	D	Eb	F	G	A	B

        [min 2nd] [min 2nd]

Copyright 2013 by Kevin G. Pace
PaceMusicServices.com

Melodic Minor - Chords & Scales

Chords			Modes						
	min 6	minMaj 7	Mel Min						
		min 7	2	Phr #6					
		AugMaj7	3	2	Lyd Aug				
	x7	x7(#11)	4	3	2	Lyd Dom			
x7	x7(b13)	x7(#5)	5	4	3	2	Mixo b6		
	half-dim 7	half-dim 9	6	5	4	3	2	Loc #2	
half-dim 7	*Altered (any #/b 5/9)		7	6	5	4	3	2	Alt
	min 6	minMaj 7	------	7	6	5	4	3	2
		min 7	------------		7	6	5	4	3
		AugMaj7	------------------			7	6	5	4
	x7	x7(#11)	----------------------------				7	6	5
x7	x7(b13)	x7(#5)	------------------------------------					7	6
	half-dim 7	half-dim 9	---						7

(the numbers above represent the scale degrees of the various modes)

Each mode is shown with its main chord(s) to the left of its name.

Other possible chords are listed to left of the numbers. Play the chord with its root on the scale degree of the number to its left.

> For example: let's say you are playing a C Locrian #2 scale (C-D-Eb-F-Gb-Ab-Bb-C)
>
> 1. Find the Loc #2 heading in the chart.
> 2. Look to the far left of this heading. You see that the main chords are half-dim 7 or 9 chords.
> 3. Directly under the heading of Loc #2 is the number "2". This represents the 2nd scale degree of Locrian #2. To the far left of this "2" you see half-dim 7 or Altered. Play these chords with their root on the 2nd scale degree of Locrian #2. In other words, play a D half-dim 7 chord against a C Locrian #2 scale.
> 4. Continuing down the column under the heading of Loc #2 is the number "3", representing scale degree 3 of Locrian #2. To the far left of this "3" you see minor 6 or minor-Major 7. Play either of these chord with their root on the 3rd scale degree of Locrian #2. In other words, play an Ebm6 chord against a C Locrian #2 scale.
> 5. Continue in a similar fashion on each scale degree of the Locrian #2 or any of the other modes.

*Note: the Altered Dominant chord is a dominant 7 chord with any combination of b5, #5, b9, or #9.

Examples of Alt Dom chords:
- D Dominant 7(b5): (D-F#-Ab-C)
- D Dominant b9: (D-F#-A-C-Eb)
- D Dominant 9(b5): (D-F#-Ab-C-E)
- D Dominant 7(b9/b5): (D-F#-Ab-C-Eb)
- D Dominant 7(#9/b5): (D-F#-Ab-C-E#)
- D Dominant 7(#5): (D-F#-A#-C)
- D Dominant #9: (D-F#-A-C-E#)
- D Dominant 9(#5): (D-F#-A#-C-E)
- D Dominant 7(b9/#5): (D-F#-A#-C-Eb)
- D Dominant 7(#9/#5): (D-F#-A#-C-E#)

Copyright 2013 by Kevin G. Pace
PaceMusicServices.com

Pg. 29
Harmonic Minor Scale

Harmonic Minor is the parent scale of several modes, covered in the next pages.
It could be thought of as Aeolian #7.
It is an Aeolian (Natural Minor) scale with a sharped 7 scale degree.
    Example: A Harmonic Minor is the same as A Aeolian, but with G#
      (See below under ways to think about the scale).

Interesting or defining features:
Augmented 2nd between scale degrees 6 & 7.
Minor 2nds between scale degrees 2 & 3, 5 & 6, 7 & 8

Chords that may be used with this scale: (examples in C Harmonic Minor)
Minor triad (C-Eb-G)
Minor-Major 7 (C-Eb-G-B)
Minor-Major 9 (C-Eb-G-B-D)

Here are two ways to think about the Harmonic Minor scale:
1-Compare it to other scales

	A	B	C	D	E	F	G	A
A Aeolian:	A	B	C	D	E	F	G	A
A Harmonic Minor:	A	B	C	D	E	F	G#	A

Note the differences all occur on scale degree 7. Why?
Harmonic Minor is Aeolian with a Sharped (raised) 7th scale degree

2-Think of the intervals between scale degrees
    For example:

C Harmonic Minor: A B C D E F G# A
- A to B: Major 2nd
- B to C: minor 2nd
- C to D: Major 2nd
- D to E: Major 2nd
- E to F: minor 2nd
- F to G#: Aug 2nd
- G# to A: minor 2nd

Here are the 12 Harmonic Minor scales:

Half-steps between notes:
2-1-2-2-1-3-1

C	D	Eb	F	G	Ab	B	C
C#	D#	E	F#	G#	A	B#	C#
D	E	F	G	A	Bb	C#	D
Eb	F	Gb	Ab	Bb	Cb	D	Eb
E	F#	G	A	B	C	D#	E
F	G	Ab	Bb	C	Db	E	F
F#	G#	A	B	C#	D	E#	F#
G	A	Bb	C	D	Eb	F#	G
Ab	Bb	Cb	Db	Eb	Fb	G	Ab
A	B	C	D	E	F	G#	A
Bb	C	Db	Eb	F	Gb	A	Bb
B	C#	D	E	F#	G	A#	B

min 2nd intervals occur between columns 2-3, 5-6, 7-8
Aug 2nd interval occurs between columns 6-7

Copyright 2013 by Kevin G. Pace
PaceMusicServices.com

Locrian #6

2nd mode of Harmonic Minor
Parent mode: Major 2nd below 1st scale degree. Or 7th note of Locrian #6 scale.
    For example: B Locrian #6 is the 2nd mode of A Harmonic Minor.
        (See #2 under ways to think about the scale)

Interesting or defining features:
Minor 2nds between scale degrees 1 & 2, 4 & 5, 6 & 7
Augmented 2nd between scale degrees 5 & 6

Chords that may be used with this scale: (examples in C Locrian #6)
Diminished triad (C-Eb-Gb)
Half-diminished 7 (C-Eb-Gb-Bb)

Here are two ways to think about the Locrian #6 scale:
1-Compare it to other scales
    For example:

B Aeolian	B	**C#**	D	E	**F#**	G	A	B
B Locrian	B	**C**	D	E	**F**	**G**	A	B
B Locrian #6:	B	C	D	E	F	**G#**	A	B

    Note the differences all occur on scale degrees 2, 5 & 6. Why?
    Locrian is Natural Minor with flatted (lowered) 2nd & 5th scale degrees
    Locrian #6 is, as the name implies, a Locrian scale with a sharped (raised) 6th scale degree

2-Think of the notes of the parent scale and invert it
    For example:

A Harmonic Minor:	A	B	C	D	E	F	G#	A
B Locrian #6:	B	C	D	E	F	G#	A	B

Here are the 12 Locrian #6 scales:
Half-steps between notes:
    1-2-2-1-3-1-2

				Aug 2nd			
C	Db	Eb	F	Gb	A	Bb	C
C#	D	E	F#	G	A#	B	C#
D	Eb	F	G	Ab	B	C	D
D#	E	F#	G#	A	B#	C#	D#
E	F	G	A	Bb	C#	D	E
F	Gb	Ab	Bb	Cb	D	Eb	F
F#	G	A	B	C	D#	E	F#
G	Ab	Bb	C	Db	E	F	G
G#	A	B	C#	D	E#	F#	G#
A	Bb	C	D	Eb	F#	G	A
A#	B	C#	D#	E	Fx	G#	A#
B	C	D	E	F	G#	A	B
min 2nd			min 2nd		min 2nd		

Ionian #5

3rd mode of Harmonic Minor
Parent mode: Minor 3rd below 1st scale degree. Or 6th note of Ionian #5 scale.
    For example: C Ionian #5 is the 3rd mode of A Harmonic Minor.
       (See #2 under ways to think about the scale)

Interesting or defining features:
Minor 2nds between scale degrees 3 & 4, 5 & 6, 7 & 8
Augmented 2nd between scale degrees 4 & 5

Chords that may be used with this scale: (examples in C Ionian #5)
Augmented triad (C-E-G#)   Major 7(#5) (C-E-G#-B)
Dominant 7 on scale degree 3 (E-G#-B-D). In other words, play this scale a M3 below chord's root.
Dominant 7(b9/b13) on scale degree 3 (E-G#-B-D-F-C). In other words, play this scale a M3 below chord's root.

    or think this way: [Fm Triad / E7]

Here are two ways to think about the Ionian #5 scale:
1-Compare it to other scales
For example: C Ionian   C   D   E   F   **G**   A   B   C
                C Ionian #5:   C   D   E   F   **G#**   A   B   C
    Note the differences all occur on scale degree 5. Why?
    Ionian #5 is, as the name implies, a Major scale with a sharped (raised) 5th scale degree

2-Think of the notes of the parent scale and invert it
For example: A Harmonic Minor: A   B   C   D   E   F   G#   A
                C Ionian #5:   C   D   E   F   G#   A   B   C

Here are the 12 Ionian #5 scales:

Half-steps between notes: 2-2-1-3-1-2-1

			Aug 2nd			
C	D	E	F	G#	A	B	C
Db	Eb	F	Gb	A	Bb	C	Db
D	E	F#	G	A#	B	C#	D
Eb	F	G	Ab	B	C	D	Eb
E	F#	G#	A	B#	C#	D#	E
F	G	A	Bb	C#	D	E	F
Gb	Ab	Bb	Cb	D	Eb	F	Gb
G	A	B	C	D#	E	F#	G
Ab	Bb	C	Db	E	F	G	Ab
A	B	C#	D	E#	F#	G#	A
Bb	C	D	Eb	F#	G	A	Bb
B	C#	D#	E	Fx	G#	A#	B

                         min 2nd   min 2nd   min 2nd

Dorian #4

4th mode of Harmonic Minor
Parent mode: Perfect 4th below 1st scale degree. Or 5th note of Dorian #4 scale.
    For example: D Dorian #4 is the 4th mode of A Harmonic Minor.
      (See #2 under ways to think about the scale)

Interesting or defining features:
Minor 2nds between scale degrees 2 & 3, 4 & 5, 6 & 7
Augmented 2nd between scale degrees 3 & 4

Chords that may be used with this scale: (examples in C Dorian #4)
Minor 7 (C-Eb-G-Bb)   Diminished 7 (C-Eb-F#-A)
Minor 6 (C-Eb-G-A)
Dominant 7 on scale degree 2 (D-F#-A-C). In other words, play Dorian #4 scale starting a M2
    below the chord's root. (In this example, C is a M2 below the D Dominant 7's root).

Here are two ways to think about the Dorian #4 scale:

1-Compare it to other scales
    For example:

D Aeolian	D	E	F	G	A	**Bb**	C	D
D Dorian	D	E	F	**G**	A	**B**	C	D
D Dorian #4:	D	E	F	**G#**	A	B	C	D

    Note the differences all occur on scale degree 4 & 6. Why?
    Dorian is like Aeolian with a sharped (raised) 6th scale degree.
    Dorian #4 is, as the name implies, a Dorian scale with a sharped (raised) 4th scale degree.

2-Think of the notes of the parent scale and invert it
    For example:

A Harmonic Minor:	A	B	C	D	E	F	G#	A
D Dorian #4:	D	E	F	G#	A	B	C	D

Here are the 12 Dorian #4 scales:

Half-steps between notes:
2-1-3-1-2-1-2

			Aug 2nd				
C	D	Eb	F#	G	A	Bb	C
C#	D#	E	Fx	G#	A#	B	C#
D	E	F	G#	A	B	C	D
Eb	F	Gb	A	Bb	C	Db	Eb
E	F#	G	A#	B	C#	D	E
F	G	Ab	B	C	D	Eb	F
F#	G#	A	B#	C#	D#	E	F#
G	A	Bb	C#	D	E	F	G
Ab	Bb	Cb	D	Eb	F	Gb	Ab
A	B	C	D#	E	F#	G	A
Bb	C	Db	E	F	G	Ab	Bb
B	C#	D	E#	F#	G#	A	B

min 2nd   min 2nd   min 2nd

Copyright 2013 by Kevin G. Pace
PaceMusicServices.com

Phrygian #3

5th mode of Harmonic Minor. Sometimes called Spanish Phrygian.
Parent mode: Perfect 5th below 1st scale degree. Or 4th note of Phrygian #3 scale.
For example: E Phrygian #3 is the 5th mode of A Harmonic Minor. (See #2 under ways to think about the scale)

Interesting or defining features:
Minor 2nds between scale degrees 1 & 2, 3 & 4, 5 & 6
Augmented 2nd between scale degrees 2 & 3

Chords that may be used with this scale: (examples in C Phrygian #3)
Dominant 7 (C-E-G-Bb) or Dominant 7 sus (C-F-G-Bb)
Major triad on 2nd degree of Phrygian #3 (Db-F-Ab)
Major 7(b5) on 2nd scale degree (Db-F-G-C). In other words, play a Phrygian #3 scale starting on the note a
    m2 below the chord's root (in this example, C is a m2 below the chord's root of Db).
Half diminished 7 on 5th scale degree (G-Bb-Db-F). In other words, play a Phrygian #3 scale starting on the note
    a P4 up from the chord's root.
A common chord progression in Phrygian #3 is I-bII-bIII (C triad, Db triad, Eb triad).
    (The Eb triad works because even though Eb is not in the scale, its other two notes are).

Here are two ways to think about the Phrygian #3 scale:
1-Compare it to other scales
    For example:

E Aeolian	E	**F#**	G	A	B	C	D	E
E Phrygian	E	**F**	**G**	A	B	C	D	E
E Phrygian #3:	E	F	**G#**	A	B	C	D	E

Note the differences all occur on scale degree 2 & 3. Why?
Phrygian is like Aeolian with a flatted (lowered) 2nd scale degree.
Phrygian #3 is, as the name implies, a Phrygian scale with a sharped (raised) 3rd scale degree.

2-Think of the notes of the parent scale and invert it
For example:

A Harmonic Minor:	A	B	C	D	E	F	G#	A
E Phrygian #3:	E	F	G#	A	B	C	D	E

Here are the 12 Phrygian #3 scales:

Half-steps between notes:
1-3-1-2-1-2-2

		Aug 2nd					
C	Db	E	F	G	Ab	Bb	C
C#	D	E#	F#	G#	A	B	C#
D	Eb	F#	G	A	Bb	C	D
D#	E	Fx	G#	A#	B	C#	D#
E	F	G#	A	B	C	D	E
F	Gb	A	Bb	C	Db	Eb	F
F#	G	A#	B	C#	D	E	F#
G	Ab	B	C	D	Eb	F	G
G#	A	B#	C#	D#	E	F#	G#
A	Bb	C#	D	E	F	G	A
Bb	Cb	D	Eb	F	Gb	Ab	Bb
B	C	D#	E	F#	G	A	B
	min 2nd		min 2nd		min 2nd		

Copyright 2013 by Kevin G. Pace
PaceMusicServices.com

Lydian #2

6th mode of Harmonic Minor.
Parent mode: Minor 6th below 1st scale degree. Or 3rd note of Lydian #2 scale.
    For example: F Lydian #2 is the 6th mode of A Harmonic Minor.
      (See #2 under ways to think about the scale)

Interesting or defining features:
Minor 2nds between scale degrees 2 & 3, 4 & 5, 7 & 8
Augmented 2nd between scale degrees 1 & 2

Chords that may be used with this scale: (examples in C Lydian #2)
Major 7 (C-E-G-B)
Major 9 (C-E-G-B-D). Even though D isn't part of the scale, this chord still sounds good.
Major 7(b5) (C-E-Gb-B or C-E-F#-B)

Here are two ways to think about the Lydian #2 scale:
1-Compare it to other scales
    For example:

F Ionian (Major)	F	G	A	**Bb**	C	D	E	F
F Lydian	F	**G**	A	**B**	C	D	E	F
F Lydian #2	F	**G#**	A	B	C	D	E	F

Note the differences all occur on scale degree 2 & 4. Why?
Lydian is like Ionian with a sharped (raised) 4th scale degree.
Lydian #2 is, as the name implies, a Lydian scale with a sharped (raised) 2nd scale degree.

2-Think of the notes of the parent scale and invert it
    For example:

A Harmonic Minor:	A	B	C	D	E	F	G#	A
F Lydian #2:	F	G#	A	B	C	D	E	F

Here are the 12 Lydian #2 scales:

Half-steps between notes:
3-1-2-1-2-2-1

Aug 2nd						
C	D#	E	F#	G	A	B	C
Db	E	F	G	Ab	Bb	C	Db
D	E#	F#	G#	A	B	C#	D
Eb	F#	G	A	Bb	C	D	Eb
E	Fx	G#	A#	B	C#	D#	E
F	G#	A	B	C	D	E	F
Gb	A	Bb	C	Db	Eb	F	Gb
G	A#	B	C#	D	E	F#	G
Ab	B	C	D	Eb	F	G	Ab
A	B#	C#	D#	E	F#	G#	A
Bb	C#	D	E	F	G	A	Bb
B	Cx	D#	E#	F#	G#	A#	B

min 2nd   min 2nd   min 2nd

Copyright 2013 by Kevin G. Pace
PaceMusicServices.com

Altered b7

7th mode of Harmonic Minor.
Parent mode: Major 7th below 1st scale degree. Or 2nd note of Altered b7 scale.
For example: G# Altered b7 is the 7th mode of A Harmonic Minor.
(See #2 under ways to think about the scale)

Interesting or defining features:
Minor 2nds between scale degrees 1 & 2, 3 & 4, 6 & 7
Augmented 2nd between scale degrees 7 & 8

Chords that may be used with this scale: (examples in C Altered b7)
Fully Diminished 7 (C-Eb-Gb-Bbb)

Here are three ways to think about the Altered b7 scale:
1-Compare it to other scales
For example:

B minor	B	**C#**	D	E	**F#**	G	A	B
B Locrian	B	**C**	D	**E**	**F**	G	**A**	B
B Altered b7	B	C	D	**Eb**	F	G	**Ab**	B

Note the differences all occur on scale degree 2, 4, 5 & 7. Why?
Locrian is like Aeolian with flatted (lowered) 2nd & 5th scale degree.
Altered b7 is a Locrian scale with a flatted (lowered) 4th & 7th scale degrees.

2-Think of the notes of the parent scale and invert it
For example: A Harmonic Minor: A   B   C   D   E   F   G#   A
G# Altered b7:   G#   A   B   C   D   E   F   G#

3-Compare to the Altered Scale (see 7th mode of Melodic Minor)
C Altered: C   Db   D#   E   Gb   G#   Bb   C
C Altered b7   C   Db   D#   E   Gb   G#   Bbb   C

Altered b7 is the same as the Altered Scale with a lowered 7th scale degree.

Here are the 12 Altered b7 scales:

Half-steps between notes:
1-2-1-2-2-1-3

						Aug 2nd	
C	Db	Eb	Fb	Gb	Ab	Bbb	C
C#	D	E	F	G	A	Bb	C#
D	Eb	F	Gb	Ab	Bb	Cb	D
D#	E	F#	G	A	B	C	D#
E	F	G	Ab	Bb	C	Db	E
E#	F#	G#	A	B	C#	D	E#
F#	G	A	Bb	C	D	Eb	F#
G	Ab	Bb	Cb	Db	Eb	Fb	G
G#	A	B	C	D	E	F	G#
A	Bb	C	Db	Eb	F	Gb	A
A#	B	C#	D	E	F#	G	A#
B	C	D	Eb	F	G	Ab	B
min 2nd		min 2nd			min 2nd		

Copyright 2013 by Kevin G. Pace
PaceMusicServices.com

Pg. 36

Harmonic Minor - Chords & Scales

Chords			Modes						
Minor Triad	Min-Maj 7	Min-Maj 9	Harm Min						
Dim Triad	Half-dim 7		2	Loc #6					
Aug Triad	Aug Maj 7		3	2	Ion #5				
Minor Triad	Minor 7	Minor 9	4	3	2	Dor #4			
Dominant 7	Dominant b9	Dom 7 (b9/b13)	5	4	3	2	Phry #3		
Major Triad	Major 7	Major 7 (#11)	6	5	4	3	2	Lyd #2	
Dim Triad	Fully Dim 7		7	6	5	4	3	2	Alt b7
Minor Triad	Min-Maj 7	Min-Maj 9	--------	7	6	5	4	3	2
Dim Triad	Half-dim 7				7	6	5	4	3
Aug Triad	Aug Maj 7					7	6	5	4
Minor Triad	Minor 7	Minor 9					7	6	5
Dominant 7	Dominant b9	Dom 7 (b9/b13)						7	6
Major Triad	Major 7	Major 7 (#11)							7

Note: #11 is the same note as b5.
b13 is the same note as #5.

(The numbers above represent the scale degrees of the various modes on which you can build the chords shown in the columns to their left).

Each mode is shown with its main chord(s) to the left of its name.

Other possible chords are listed to left of the numbers. Play the chord with its root on the scale degree of the number to its left.

Example: Let's say you are playing a C Ionian #5 scale (C-D-E-F-G#-A-B-C)

1. Find the Ionian #5 heading in the chart.
2. Look to the far left of this heading. You see that the main chords are Augmented Triad or Augmented Major 7.
3. Directly under the heading of Ionian is the number "2". This represents the 2nd scale degree of Ionian #5. To the far left of this "2" you see Minor Triad, Minor 7, or Minor 9. Play these chords with their roots on the 2nd degree of Ionian #5. In other words, play a D minor 7 chord against a C Ionian #5 scale.
4. Continuing down the column under the heading of Ionian #5 is the number "3", representing scale degree 3 of Ionian #5. To the far left of this "3" you see Dom 7, Dom 7(b9), and Dom 7 (b9/b13). Play any of these chords with their root on the 3rd scale degree of Ionian #5. In other words, play an E Dominant 7 (b9) against a C Ionian #5 scale.
5. Continue in a similar fashion on each scale degree of any of the other modes.

Example #2: Play the C Phrygian #3 mode (C-Db-E-F-G-Ab-Bb-C)

1. Find the Phrygian heading in the chart.
2. Look to the far left of this heading. You see that the main chords are Dom 7, Dom 7(b9), and Dom 7 (b9/b13).
3. Go down below Phrygian #3's heading to the number "3". This represents the 3rd scale degree of Phrygian #3. To the far left of this "3" you see Diminished Triad or Fully Diminished 7. Play these chords with their root on the 3rd scale degree of Phrygian #3. In other words, play a E fully diminished 7 chord against a C Phrygian #3 scale.

Copyright 2013 by Kevin G. Pace
PaceMusicServices.com

Harmonic Major (Ionian b6)

Harmonic Major is the parent scale of several modes, covered in the next pages.
It is a Major scale with a flatted (lowered) 6th scale degree.
Example: C Harmonic Major is the same as C Major, but with Ab as the 6th scale degree.
(See #2 under ways to think about the scale)

Interesting or defining features:
Augmented 2nd between scale degrees 6 & 7
Minor 2nds between scale degrees 3 & 4, 5 & 6, 7 & 8

Chords that may be used with this scale: (examples in C Harmonic Major)
Major 7 (C-E-G-B)
Major b6 (C-E-G-Ab) or Major 7(b13) (C-E-G-Ab-B). Enharmonically, this is also C augmented (C-E-G#).
Major 9 (C-E-G-B-D)

Here are two ways to think about the Harmonic Major scale:
1-Compare it to other scales
    For example:
        C Major (Ionian)   C   D   E   F   G   **A**   B   C
        C Harmonic Major   C   D   E   F   G   **Ab**   B   C

    Note the difference at scale degree 6. Why?
    Harmonic Major is just a major scale with a flat (lowered) 6th scale degree

2-Think of the notes of the Major scale and flat the 6th scale degree
    For example:
        C Major (Ionian)   C   D   E   F   G   **A**   B   C
        C Harmonic Major   C   D   E   F   G   **Ab**   B   C

Here are the 12 Harmonic Major scales:

Half-steps between notes:
2-2-1-2-1-3-1

					Aug 2nd		
C	D	E	F	G	Ab	B	C
Db	Eb	F	Gb	Ab	Bbb	C	Db
D	E	F#	G	A	Bb	C#	D
Eb	F	G	Ab	Bb	Cb	D	Eb
E	F#	G#	A	B	C	D#	E
F	G	A	Bb	C	Db	E	F
F#	G#	A#	B	C#	D	E#	F#
G	A	B	C	D	Eb	F#	G
Ab	Bb	C	Db	Eb	Fb	G	Ab
A	B	C#	D	E	F	G#	A
Bb	C	D	Eb	F	Gb	A	Bb
B	C#	D#	E	F#	G	A#	B

min 2nd / min 2nd / min 2nd

Copyright 2013 by Kevin G. Pace
PaceMusicServices.com

Dorian b5

2nd mode of Harmonic Major
Parent mode: Major 2nd below 1st scale degree. Or 7th note of Dorian b5 scale.
    For example: D Dorian b5 is the 2nd mode of C Harmonic Major.
        (See #2 under ways to think about the scale)

Interesting or defining features:
Augmented 2nd between scale degrees 5 & 6
Minor 2nds between scale degrees 2 & 3, 4 & 5, 6 & 7

Chords that may be used with this scale: (examples in C Dorian b5)
Diminished triad (C-Eb-Gb)   Fully-diminished 7 (C-Eb-Gb-Bbb)
Half-diminished 7 (C-Eb-Gb-Bb)
Dominant 7 sus4 (built on 4th note of scale (F-Bb-C-Eb). In other words, play the Dorian b5 starting
    on the note a P5 above the chord's root (in this example, C is a P5 above the chord's root).

Here are two ways to think about the Dorian b5 scale:
1-Compare it to other scales
    For example:

D Natural Minor:	D	E	F	G	**A**	**Bb**	C	D
D Dorian:	D	E	F	G	**A**	**B**	C	D
D Dorian b5:	D	E	F	G	**Ab**	**B**	C	D

Note the differences all occur on scale degrees 5 & 6. Why?
Dorian is Natural Minor with a sharped (raised) 6th scale degree
Dorian b5 is, as the name implies, a Dorian scale with a flatted (lowered) 5th scale degree

2-Think of the notes of the parent scale and invert it

For example: C Harmonic Major:	C	D	E	F	G	Ab	B	C	
D Dorian b5:		D	E	F	G	Ab	B	C	D

Here are the 12 Dorian b5 scales:

Half-steps between notes: 2-1-2-1-3-1-2

				Aug 2nd		
C	D	Eb	F	Gb	A	Bb	C
C#	D#	E	F#	G	A#	B	C#
D	E	F	G	Ab	B	C	D
Eb	F	Gb	Ab	Bbb	C	Db	Eb
E	F#	G	A	Bb	C#	D	E
F	G	Ab	Bb	Cb	D	Eb	F
F#	G#	A	B	C	D#	E	F#
G	A	Bb	C	Db	E	F	G
G#	A#	B	C#	D	E#	F#	G#
A	B	C	D	Eb	F#	G	A
Bb	C	Db	Eb	Fb	G	Ab	Bb
B	C#	D	E	F	G#	A	B

min 2nd   min 2nd   min 2nd

Copyright 2013 by Kevin G. Pace
PaceMusicServices.com

Phrygian b4

3rd mode of Harmonic Major
Parent mode: Major 3rd below 1st scale degree. Or 6th note of Phrygian b4 scale.
    For example: E Phrygian is the 3rd mode of C Harmonic Major.
        (See #2 under ways to think about the scale)

Interesting or defining features:
Augmented 2nd between scale degrees 4 & 5.
Minor 2nds between scale degrees 1 & 2, 3 & 4, 5 & 6

Chords that may be used with this scale: (examples in C Phrygian b4)
Dominant 7 (C-E-G-Bb)   Dominant 7(#5) (C-Eb-G#-Bb)
Minor 7 (C-Eb-G-Bb)   Dominant 7sus4(b9) (C-F-G-Bb-Db)
Major 7b5 chord a half-step above the tonic: (Db-F-Abb-C). In other words, play a Phrygian b4 scale
    on the note a m2 below the chord's root (in this example, C is a m2 below the chord's root).

Here are two ways to think about the Phrygian b4 mode:
1-Compare it to another scale
    For example:

E Natural Minor:	E	**F#**	G	A	B	C	D	E
E Phrygian:	E	**F**	G	**A**	B	C	D	E
E Phrygian b4:	E	F	G	**Ab**	B	C	D	E

Note the difference on scale degrees 2 & 4. Phrygian b4 has lowered 2nd & 4th scale degrees.

2-Think of the notes of the parent scale and invert it
    For example:

C Harmonic Major:	C	D	E	F	G	**Ab**	B	C
E Phrygian b4:	E	F	G	**Ab**	B	C	D	E

Here are the 12 Phrygian b4 scales
Half-steps between notes:
    1-2-1-3-1-2-2

	min 2nd		min 2nd		min 2nd		
C	Db	Eb	Fb	G	Ab	Bb	C
C#	D	E	F	G#	A	B	C#
D	Eb	F	Gb	A	Bb	C	D
D#	E	F#	G	A#	B	C#	D#
E	F	G	Ab	B	C	D	E
F	Gb	Ab	Bbb	C	Db	Eb	F
F#	G	A	Bb	C#	D	E	F#
G	Ab	Bb	Cb	D	Eb	F	G
G#	A	B	C	D#	E	F#	G#
A	Bb	C	Db	E	F	G	A
Bb	Cb	Db	Ebb	F	Gb	Ab	Bb
B	C	D	Eb	F#	G	A	B
			Aug 2nd				

Alternate spelling for Bb Phrygian b4:   A#   B   C#   D   E#   F#   G#   A#

Copyright 2013 by Kevin G. Pace
PaceMusicServices.com

(see alternate spelling below)

Lydian b3

4th mode of Harmonic Major
Parent mode: Perfect 4th below 1st scale degree. Or 5th note of Lydian b3 scale.
    For example: C Lydian b3 is the 4th mode of G Harmonic Major.
       (See #2 under ways to think about the scale)

Interesting or defining features:
Same as Major with flatted 3rd & sharped 4th scale degrees.
Augmented 2nd between scale degrees 3 & 4
Minor 2nds between scale degrees 2 & 3, 4 & 5, 7 & 8

Chords that may be used with this scale: (examples in C Lydian b3)
Minor-Major 7 (C-Eb-G-B)
Minor-Major 7(b5) (C-Eb-Gb-B)

Here are two ways to think about the Lydian b3 mode:
1-Compare it to another scale
    For example:

F Major (Ionian)	F	G	**A**	**Bb**	C	D	E	F
F Lydian	F	G	**A**	**B**	C	D	E	F
F Lydian b3	F	G	**Ab**	**B**	C	D	E	F

Note the differences on scale degrees 3 & 4.
Lydian b3 is like major with lowered 3rd & raised 4th scale degrees.

2-Think of the notes of the parent scale and invert it
    For example:

G Harmonic Major:	G	A	B	C	D	Eb	F#	G
C Lydian b3	C	D	Eb	F#	G	A	B	C

Here are the 12 Lydian b3 scales:

Half-steps between notes:
2-1-3-1-2-2-1

		Aug 2nd				
C	D	Eb	F#	G	A	B	C
Db	Eb	Fb	G	Ab	Bb	C	Db
D	E	F	G#	A	B	C#	D
Eb	F	Gb	A	Bb	C	D	Eb
E	F#	G	A#	B	C#	D#	E
F	G	Ab	B	C	D	E	F
F#	G#	A	B#	C#	D#	E#	F#
G	A	Bb	C#	D	E	F#	G
Ab	Bb	Cb	D	Eb	F	G	Ab
A	B	C	D#	E	F#	G#	A
Bb	C	Db	E	F	G	A	Bb
B	C#	D	E#	F#	G#	A#	B
	min 2nd		min 2nd			min 2nd	

Copyright 2013 by Kevin G. Pace
PaceMusicServices.com

Mixolydian b2

5th mode of Harmonic Major
Parent mode: Perfect 5th below 1st scale degree. Or 4th note of Mixolydian b2 scale.
    For example: G Mixolydian b2 is the 5th mode of C Harmonic Major.
      (See #2 under ways to think about the scale)

Interesting or defining features:
Same as Major with flatted 2nd & 7th scale degrees.
Augmented 2nd between scale degrees 2 & 3
Minor 2nds between scale degrees 1 & 2, 3 & 4, 6 & 7

Chords that may be used with this scale: (examples in C Mixolydian b2)
Dominant 7 (C-E-G-Bb)   Dominant 7(b9) (C-E-G-Bb-Db)

Here are two ways to think about the Mixolydian b2 mode:
1-Compare it to another scale

For example: G Major (Ionian)	G	A	B	C	D	E	**F#**	G
G Mixolydian	G	**A**	B	C	D	E	**F**	G
G Mixolydian b2	G	**Ab**	B	C	D	E	F	G

Note the differences on scale degrees 2 & 7.
Mixolydian is like Ionian with a lowered 7th scale degree
Mixolydian b2 is like Mixolydian with lowered 2nd scale degree.

2-Think of the notes of the parent scale and invert it

For example: C Harmonic Major:	C	D	E	F	G	Ab	B	C
G Mixolydian b2	G	Ab	B	C	D	E	F	G

Here are the 12 Mixolydian b2 scales:

		Aug 2nd					
C	Db	E	F	G	A	Bb	C
C#	D	E#	F#	G#	A#	B	C#
D	Eb	F#	G	A	B	C	D
Eb	Fb	G	Ab	Bb	C	Db	Eb
E	F	G#	A	B	C#	D	E
F	Gb	A	Bb	C	D	Eb	F
F#	G	A#	B	C#	D#	E	F#
G	Ab	B	C	D	E	F	G
G#	A	B#	C#	D#	E#	F#	G#
A	Bb	C#	D	E	F#	G	A
Bb	Cb	D	Eb	F	G	Ab	Bb
B	C	D#	E	F#	G#	A	B

(See alternate spelling below for C# and G#)

Half-steps between notes:
    1-3-1-2-2-1-2

min 2nd columns: between 1-2, 3-4, 6-7

| Alternate spelling of C#: | Db | Ebb | F | Gb | Ab | Bb | Cb | Db |
| Alternate spelling of G#: | Ab | Bbb | C | Db | Eb | F | Gb | Ab |

Copyright 2013 by Kevin G. Pace
PaceMusicServices.com

Lydian Augmented #2

6th mode of Harmonic Major
Parent mode: Minor 6th below 1st scale degree. Or 3rd note of Lydian Augmented #2 scale.
    For example: Ab Lydian Augmented #2 is the 6th mode of C Harmonic Major.
      (See #2 under ways to think about the scale)

Interesting or defining features:
Same as Major with sharped 2nd, 4th, & 5th scale degrees.
Augmented 2nd between scale degrees 1 & 2
Minor 2nds between scale degrees 2 & 3, 5 & 6, 7 & 8

Chords that may be used with this scale: (examples in C Lydian Augmented #2)
Major 7(#5) (C-E-G#-B)

Here are two ways to think about the Lydian Augmented #2 mode:
1-Compare it to another scale
    For example:

F Major (Ionian):	F	G	A	**Bb**	C	D	E	F
F Lydian:	F	**G**	A	**B**	**C**	D	E	F
F Lydian Augmented #2:	F	**G#**	A	B	**C#**	D	E	F

Note the differences on scale degrees 2, 4, & 5.
Lydian is like Ionian with a raised 4th scale degree
Lydian Augmented #2 is like Lydian with raised 2nd & 5th scale degrees.

2-Think of the notes of the parent scale and invert it
    For example:

C Harmonic Major:	C	D	E	F	G	Ab	B	C
Ab Lydian Augmented #2:	Ab	B	C	D	E	F	G	Ab

Here are the 12 Lydian Augmented #2 scales:

	Aug 2nd						
	C	D#	E	F#	G#	A	B	C
Half-steps between notes:	Db	E	F	G	A	Bb	C	Db
3-1-2-2-1-2-1	D	E#	F#	G#	A#	B	C#	D
	Eb	F#	G	A	B	C	D	Eb
(See alternate spelling below)	Fb	G	Ab	Bb	C	Db	Eb	Fb
	F	G#	A	B	C#	D	E	F
	Gb	A	Bb	C	D	Eb	F	Gb
	G	A#	B	C#	D#	E	F#	G
	Ab	B	C	D	E	F	G	Ab
	A	B#	C#	D#	E#	F#	G#	A
	Bb	C#	D	E	F#	G	A	Bb
(See alternate spelling below)	Cb	D	Eb	F	G	Ab	Bb	Cb
		min 2nd			min 2nd		min 2nd	
Alternate spelling of Fb:	E	Fx	G#	A#	B#	C#	D#	E
Alternate spelling of Cb:	B	Cx	D#	E#	Fx	G#	A#	B

Copyright 2013 by Kevin G. Pace
PaceMusicServices.com

Locrian b7

7th mode of Harmonic Major
Parent mode: Major 7th below 1st scale degree. Or 2nd note of Locrian b7 scale.
    For example: B Locrian b7 is the 7th mode of C Harmonic Major.
        (See #2 under ways to think about the scale)

Interesting or defining features:
Same as minor with flatted 2nd, 5th, & 7th scale degrees.
Augmented 2nd between scale degrees 7 & 8
Minor 2nds between scale degrees 1 & 2, 4 & 5, 6 & 7

Chords that may be used with this scale: (examples in C Locrian b7)
Fully Diminished 7 (C-Eb-Gb-Bbb). Note: Bbb = A.

Here are two ways to think about the Locrian b7 mode:
1-Compare it to another scale
    For example:

	1	2	3	4	5	6	7	8
B minor (Aeolian):	B	**C#**	D	E	**F#**	G	A	B
B Locrian:	B	**C**	D	E	**F**	G	**A**	B
F Locrian b7:	B	C	D	E	F	G	**Ab**	B

Note the differences on scale degrees 2, 5, & 7.
Locrian is like Aeolian with a lowered 2nd & 5th scale degrees.
Locrian b7 is, as the name implies, Locrian with a lowered 7th scale degree.

2-Think of the notes of the parent scale and invert it
    For example:

C Harmonic Major:	C	D	E	F	G	Ab	B	C
B Locrian b7:	B	C	D	E	F	G	Ab	B

Here are the 12 Locrian b7 scales:

Half-steps between notes: 1-2-2-1-2-1-3

						Aug 2nd	
C	Db	Eb	F	Gb	Ab	Bbb	C
C#	D	E	F#	G	A	Bb	C#
D	Eb	F	G	Ab	Bb	Cb	D
D#	E	F#	G#	A	B	C	D#
E	F	G	A	Bb	C	Db	E
E#	F#	G#	A#	B	C#	D	E#
F#	G	A	B	C	D	Eb	F#
G	Ab	Bb	C	Db	Eb	Fb	G
G#	A	B	C#	D	E	F	G#
A	Bb	C	D	Eb	F	Gb	A
A#	B	C#	D#	E	F#	G	A#
B	C	D	E	F	G	Ab	B
min 2nd		min 2nd		min 2nd		

(See alternate spelling below)

Copyright 2013 by Kevin G. Pace
PaceMusicServices.com

(See alternate spelling below)

| Alternate spelling for E#: | F | Gb | Ab | Bb | Cb | Db | Ebb | F |
| Alternate spelling for A#: | Bb | Cb | Db | Eb | Fb | Gb | Abb | Bb |

Harmonic Major - Chords & Scales

Chords			Modes						
Major 7	Major 7 (#5)		Harm Maj						
Half-dim 7			2	Dor b5					
Minor Triad	Minor 7	Dom 7 (#9)	3	2	Phry b4				
Minor Triad	Min-Maj 7		4	3	2	Lydian b3			
Dominant 7	Dominant b9	Dom13 (b9)	5	4	3	2	Mixo b2		
Major 7 (#5)			6	5	4	3	2	Lyd-Aug #2	
Dim Triad	Fully Dim 7		7	6	5	4	3	2	Loc b7
Major 7	Major 7 (#5)			7	6	5	4	3	2
Half-dim 7	Fully-dim 7				7	6	5	4	3
Minor Triad	Dom 7 (#9)					7	6	5	4
Minor Triad	Min-Maj 7	Min-Maj 7(b5)					7	6	5
Dominant 7	Dominant b9	Dom13 (b9)						7	6
Major 7 (#5)									7

(The numbers above represent the scale degrees of the various modes on which you can build the chords shown in the columns to their left).

Each mode is shown with its main chord(s) to the left of its name.

Other possible chords are listed to left of the numbers. Play the chord with its root on the scale degree of the number to its left.

Example: Let's say you are playing a D Dorian b5 scale (D-E-F-G-Ab-B-C-D).

1. Find the Dorian b5 heading in the chart.
2. Look to the far left of this heading. You see that the main chord is the half-diminished 7 chord.
3. Directly under the heading of Dorian b5 is the number "2". This represents the 2nd scale degree of Dorian b5. To the far left of this "2" you see Minor Triad, Minor 7, or Dom 7(#9). Play these chords with their roots on the 2nd degree of Dorian b5. In other words, play an E minor 7 chord against a D Dorian b5 scale.
4. Continuing down the column under the heading of Dorian b5 is the number "3", representing scale degree 3 of Dorian b5. To the far left of this "3" you see Minor Triad or Minor-Major 7 chord. Play either of these chords with their root on the 3rd scale degree of Dorian b5. In other words, play an F minor-Major 7 chord against a D Dorian b5 scale.
5. Continue in a similar fashion on each scale degree of any of the other modes.

Copyright 2013 by Kevin G. Pace
PaceMusicServices.com

Octatonic Scales

Interesting or defining features:
8 note scale that repeats the same pattern of whole and half steps throughout (1/2, whole, 1/2, whole, etc.)

Chords that may be used with these scales:
Dominant 7 chord with the half-whole scale (example: C-E-G-Bb)
Fully diminished 7 chord with whole-half scale (example: C#-E-G-Bb)

OCTATONIC HALF-WHOLE

C	Db	Eb	E	F#	G	A	Bb	C
C#	D	E	F	G	Ab	Bb	B	Db
D	Eb	F	Gb	Ab	A	B	C	D
Eb	E	F#	G	A	Bb	C	Db	Eb
E	F	G	Ab	Bb	B	C#	D	E
F	Gb	Ab	A	B	C	D	Eb	F
F#	G	A	Bb	C	Db	Eb	E	F#
G	Ab	Bb	B	C#	D	E	F	G
Ab	A	B	C	D	Eb	F	Gb	Ab
A	Bb	C	Db	Eb	E	F#	G	A
Bb	B	C#	D	E	F	G	Ab	Bb
B	C	D	Eb	F	Gb	Ab	A	B

OCTATONIC WHOLE-HALF

C	D	Eb	F	Gb	Ab	A	B	C
Db	Eb	E	F#	G	A	Bb	C	Db
D	E	F	G	Ab	Bb	B	C#	D
Eb	F	Gb	Ab	A	B	C	D	Eb
E	F#	G	A	Bb	C	Db	Eb	E
F	G	Ab	Bb	B	C#	D	E	F
Gb	Ab	A	B	C	D	Eb	F	Gb
G	A	Bb	C	Db	Eb	E	Gb	G
Ab	Bb	B	C#	D	E	F	G	Ab
A	B	C	D	Eb	F	Gb	Ab	A
Bb	C	Db	Eb	E	F#	G	A	Bb
B	C#	D	E	F	G	Ab	Bb	B

The 3 Octatonic Keyboard Patterns

Starting Note

Half-whole	Whole-half
C	Db
Eb	E
F#	G
A	Bb

Keyboard pattern #1: black keys: Db Eb F# Bb; white keys: C E G A C

Half-whole	Whole-half
C#	D
E	F
G	Ab
Bb	B

Keyboard pattern #2: black keys: C# Ab Bb C#; white keys: D E F G B

Half-whole	Whole-half
D	Eb
F	F#
G#	A
B	C

Keyboard pattern #3: black keys: Eb F# G#; white keys: D F A B C D

Notice these points:
*The 4 starting notes in the 2 columns above combine together to form a fully diminished 7th chord (from top down).
*Note the pattern of black and white keys in each keyboard pattern.
*It's helpful to break each 8 note scale in half. Look at patterns of the 1st 4 notes & the last 4 notes.
*There are 24 possible scales (12 starting notes with 2 different octatonic scales built on each starting note).

Try this exercise at the piano:
1) Play the C Octatonic **half-whole** scale with the RH. Play a sustained C7 chord in the LH while you play the scale.
2) Notice the pattern of white & black keys: White, black, black, white. Black, white, white, black. Then back to C.
3) Play the Eb Octatonic half-whole scale with the RH with an Eb7 chord in the LH.
    Notice the pattern of black & white keys is still the same.
4) Repeat this starting on F#, then A.
5) Repeat step 1, but play C# Octatonic **whole-half** with a C# fully dim chord in the LH.
    Notice the pattern of black & white keys is still the same.
6) Repeat the Octatonic whole-half scales starting on E, then G, and then Bb.
You will have played 8 Octatonic scales which all use the same pattern of white & black keys.
    This is keyboard pattern #1.
Now go through the above 6 steps with keyboard pattern #2 and then pattern #3.

Copyright 2013 by Kevin G. Pace
PaceMusicServices.com

Symmetrical Augmented

A 6 note scale

Interesting or defining features:
Follows the same pattern throughout: Minor 3rd, Minor 2nd, Minor 3rd, Minor 2nd, etc.

Chords that may be used with this scale: (examples in C Symmetrical Augmented)
Major 7 (C-E-G-B)
Minor-Major 7 (C-Eb-G-B)
Augmented triad 7 (C-E-G#)
Augmented Major 7 (C-E-G#-B) - most common

Here is one way to think about the Symmetrical Augmented mode:

Think of the intervals between scale degrees.
For example:

	minor 3rd		minor 3rd		minor 3rd	
		min 2nd		min 2nd		min 2nd

C Symmetrical Augmented: C D# E G Ab B C

Here are the 12 Symmetrical Augmented scales:

C	D#	E	G	Ab	B	C
C#	E	F	Ab	A	C	Db
D	F	F#	A	Bb	C#	D
D#	F#	G	A#	B	D	Eb
E	G	G#	B	C	D#	E
F	G#	A	C	Db	E	F
F#	A	Bb	Db	D	F	Gb
G	A#	B	D	Eb	F#	G
G#	B	C	Eb	E	G	Ab
A	C	Db	E	F	G#	A
A#	C#	D	F	Gb	A	Bb
B	D	D#	F#	G	A#	B

Half-steps between notes:
3-1-3-1-3-1

	minor 3rd		minor 3rd		minor 3rd	
		min 2nd		min 2nd		min 2nd

Pg. 47

Chromatic Scale

Interesting or defining features:
Uses all 12 notes
It's the same no matter where you start
When ascending, the scale is spelled with sharps. When descending, the scale is spelled with flats.
Minor 2nds between all scale degrees

Chords that may be used with this scale:
Since the chromatic scale includes all notes, any chord can be played under this scale.

Here is the Chromatic Scale:

Ascending:	C	C#	D	D#	E	F	F#	G	G#	A	A#	B	C
RH Fingering:	2	3	1	3	1	2	3	1	3	1	3	1	2
Descending:	C	B	Bb	A	Ab	G	Gb	F	E	Eb	D	Db	C
RH Fingering:	1	2	3	1	3	1	3	1	2	3	1	3	1

These fingerings work going either direction and starting at any point withing the scale.

Copyright 2013 by Kevin G. Pace
PaceMusicServices.com

Gypsy

The Gypsy scale is like an Ionian scale with a flat 2 and 6.
It is sometimes called the Double Harmonic minor scale, because of its two augmented 2nds.

Interesting or defining features:
Minor 2nds between scale degrees 1-2, 3-4, 5-6, 7-8. Augmented 2nds between degrees 2-3, 6-7.

Chords that may be used with this scale: (examples in C Gypsy)
Major triad (C-E-G)   Dominant 7 (C-E-G-Bb)
Major 7 (C-E-G-B)
Minor triad built on 4 (F-Ab-C). To think of it another way, play the C Gypsy Scale starting on the 5th
    of the F minor triad (because C is the 5th of the F minor triad).
Minor Major 7 built on 4 (F-Ab-C-E). See explanation above for Minor Triad.
Augmented triad built on 6 (Ab-C-E). To think of it another way, play the C Gypsy starting on the
    3rd of the Ab Augmented Triad (because C is the 3rd of the Ab Augmented Triad).
Augmented Major 7 built on 6 (Ab-C-E-G). See explanation above for Augmented Triad.

Here are two ways to think about the Gypsy scale:
1-Compare it to another scale
    For example:
        C Major   C   **D**   E   F   G   **A**   B   C
        C Gypsy   C   **Db**   E   F   G   **Ab**   B   C
    Note differences on scale degrees 2 & 6. The Gypsy scale is a major scale with lowered 2 & 6.

2-Think of intervals between scale degrees.
    For example: m2   A2   m2   M2   m2   A2   m2
                        (m2=minor 2nd, M2=Major 2nd, A2=Augmented 2nd)

Here are the 12 Gypsy scales:

	min 2nd		min 2nd		min 2nd		min 2nd
C	Db	E	F	G	Ab	B	C
C#	D	E#	F#	G#	A	B#	C#
D	Eb	F#	G	A	Bb	C#	D
Eb	Fb	G	Ab	Bb	Cb	D	Eb
E	F	G#	A	B	C	D#	E
F	Gb	A	Bb	C	Db	E	F
F#	G	A#	B	C#	D	E#	F#
G	Ab	B	C	D	Eb	F#	G
Ab	Bbb	C	Db	Eb	Fb	G	Ab
A	Bb	C#	D	E	F	G#	A
Bb	Cb	D	Eb	F	Gb	A	Bb
B	C	D#	E	F#	G	A#	B
		Aug 2nd				Aug 2nd	

Half-steps between notes:
    1-3-1-2-1-3-1

Copyright 2013 by Kevin G. Pace
    PaceMusicServices.com

Pg. 49

Arabian Major Scale

Considered an exotic scale, it is also called Major Locrian.
It's like the bottom half of a major scale combined with the top half of a Locrian scale.
For example: C Arabian Major = C-D-E-F (the major half) Gb-Ab-Bb-C (the Locrian half)
(See #1 under ways to think about the scale)

Interesting or defining features:
Whole tones between scale degrees 5 through 8
2 consecutive minor 2nds between scale degrees 3 & 4, 4 & 5

Chords that may be used with this scale: (examples in C Dorian b5)
Dominant 7(b5): (C-E-Gb-Bb).
Dominant 7(#5): (C-E-G#-Bb).

Here are two ways to think about the Arabian Major scale:
1-Compare it to other scales
For example:

C Major (Ionian)	C	D	E	F			
C Locrian					Gb	Ab	Bb	C
C Arabian Major	C	D	E	F	Gb	Ab	Bb	C

Arabian Major is also called Major Locrian because of the combination of Major & Locrian scales.

2-Think of the intervals between each note (W=whole step, H=half step)
For example: C Arabian Major:

	C	D	E	F	Gb	Ab	Bb	C
	W	W	H	H	W	W	W	

Here are the 12 Arabian Major scales:

Half-steps between notes:
2-2-1-1-2-2-2

C	D	E	F	Gb	Ab	Bb	C
C#	D#	E#	F#	G	A	B	C#
D	E	F#	G	Ab	Bb	C	D
Eb	F	G	Ab	Bbb	Cb	Db	Eb
E	F#	G#	A	Bb	C	D	E
F	G	A	Bb	Cb	Db	Eb	F
F#	G#	A#	B	C	D	E	F#
G	A	B	C	Db	Eb	F	G
Ab	Bb	C	Db	Ebb	Fb	Gb	Ab
A	B	C#	D	Eb	F	G	A
Bb	C	D	Eb	Fb	Gb	Ab	Bb
B	C#	D#	E	F	G	A	B

Copyright 2013 by Kevin G. Pace
PaceMusicServices.com

Harmonic Minor b2

Considered an exotic scale, it is also called the Balinese Scale or the Phrygian #7 scale.
It's like Harmonic Minor with a lowered 2nd scale degree.
   For example: C Harmonic Minor b2 = C-Db-Eb-F-G-Ab-B-C
      (See #1 under ways to think about the scale)

Interesting or defining features:
Augmented 2nd between scale degrees 6 & 7
Minor 2nds between scale degrees 1 & 2, 5 & 6, 7 & 8

Chords that may be used with this scale: (examples in C Harmonic Minor b2)
Minor-Major 7 (C-Eb-G-B).   Major 7 built on 2nd note of scale (Db-F-Ab-C).

Here are two ways to think about the Harmonic Minor b2 scale:
1-Compare it to other scales
   For example:

C Minor (Aeolian)	C	D	Eb	F	G	Ab	Bb	C
C Harmonic Minor	C	D	Eb	F	G	Ab	B	C
C Harmonic Minor b2	C	Db	Eb	F	G	Ab	B	C

   Could also be called Phrygian #7 because it's the same as Phrygian with a raised 7th scale degree.

2-Think of the intervals between each note (m2=Minor 2nd, M2=Major 2nd, A2=Augmented 2nd)
   For example: C Harm. Minor b2   C   Db   Eb   F   G   Ab   B   C
                                     m2   M2   M2   M2   m2   A2   m2

Here are the 12 Harmonic Minor b2 scales:

Half-steps between notes:
   1-2-2-2-1-3-1

	min 2nd				min 2nd		min 2nd
C	Db	Eb	F	G	Ab	B	C
C#	D	E	F#	G#	A	B#	C#
D	Eb	F	G	A	Bb	C#	D
Eb	Fb	Gb	Ab	Bb	Cb	D	Eb
E	F	G	A	B	C	D#	E
F	Gb	Ab	Bb	C	Db	E	F
F#	G	A	B	C#	D	E#	F#
G	Ab	Bb	C	D	Eb	F#	G
G#	A	B	C#	D#	E	Fx	G#
A	Bb	C	D	E	F	G#	A
Bb	Cb	Db	Eb	F	Gb	A	Bb
B	C	D	E	F#	G	A#	B

Aug 2nd

Copyright 2013 by Kevin G. Pace
PaceMusicServices.com

Hungarian Gypsy

Considered an exotic scale, it could also be called the Harmonic Minor #4 scale.
It's like Harmonic Minor with a raised 4th scale degree.
For example: C Hungarian Gypsy = C-D-Eb-F#-G-Ab-B-C
(See #1 under ways to think about the scale)

Interesting or defining features:
Augmented 2nd between scale degrees 3 & 4, 6 & 7
Minor 2nds between scale degrees 2 & 3, 4 & 5, 5 & 6, 7 & 8

Chords that may be used with this scale: (examples in C Hungarian Gypsy)
Minor-Major 7 (C-Eb-G-B). Dominant 7(b5) built on the 2nd scale degree (D-F#-Ab-C).

Here are two ways to think about the Hungarian Gypsy scale:
1-Compare it to other scales
For example:

C Minor (Aeolian)	C	D	Eb	F	G	Ab	Bb	C
C Harmonic Minor	C	D	Eb	F	G	Ab	B	C
C Hungarian Gypsy	C	D	Eb	F#	G	Ab	B	C

Could also be called Harmonic Minor #4 because it's the same as Harmonic Minor with a raised 4th scale degree.

2-Think of the intervals between each note (m2=Minor 2nd, M2=Major 2nd, A2=Augmented 2nd)

For example: C Harm. Minor b2	C	D	Eb	F#	G	Ab	B	C
	M2	m2	A2	m2	m2	A2	m2	

Here are the 12 Hungarian Gypsy scales:

Half-steps between notes: 2-1-3-1-1-3-1

	min 2nd		min 2nd	min 2nd		min 2nd	
C	D	Eb	F#	G	Ab	B	C
Db	Eb	Fb	G	Ab	Bbb	C	Db
D	E	F	G#	A	Bb	C#	D
Eb	F	Gb	A	Bb	Cb	D	Eb
E	F#	G	A#	B	C	D#	E
F	G	Ab	B	C	Db	E	F
F#	G#	A	B#	C#	D	E#	F#
G	A	Bb	C#	D	Eb	F#	G
G#	A#	B	Cx	D#	E	Fx	G#
A	B	C	D#	E	F	G#	A
Bb	C	Db	E	F	Gb	A	Bb
B	C#	D	E#	F#	G	A#	B
		Aug 2nd			Aug 2nd		

Persian

Considered an exotic scale, it could be thought of as a Locrian (#3, #7) scale.
It's like Locrian with a raised 3rd & raised 7th scale degrees.
    For example: C Persian = C-Db-E-F-Gb-Ab-B-C
       (See #1 under ways to think about the scale)

Interesting or defining features:
Augmented 2nd between scale degrees 3 & 4, 6 & 7
Minor 2nds between scale degrees 1 & 2, 3 & 4, 4 & 5, 7 & 8

Chords that may be used with this scale: (examples in C Persian)
Major 7 (b5): (C-E-Gb-B)   Major 7 (#5): (C-E-G#-B)
Major 7 built on scale degree 2 (Db-F-Ab-C)

Here are two ways to think about the Persian scale:
1-Compare it to other scales
    For example:

C Minor (Aeolian)	C	**D**	Eb	F	G	Ab	Bb	C
C Locrian	C	**Db**	**Eb**	F	Gb	Ab	**Bb**	C
C Persian	C	Db	**E**	F	Gb	Ab	**B**	C

Could also be called Locrian (#3, #7)

2-Think of the intervals between each note (m2=Minor 2nd, M2=Major 2nd, A2=Augmented 2nd)
For example: C Persian   C   Db   E   F   Gb   Ab   B   C
                            m2   A2   m2   m2   M2   A2   m2

Here are the 12 Persian scales:

Half-steps between notes:
    1-3-1-1-2-3-1

C	Db	E	F	Gb	Ab	B	C
C#	D	F	F#	G	A	C	C#
D	Eb	F#	G	Ab	Bb	C#	D
D#	E	G	G#	A	B	D	D#
E	F	G#	A	Bb	C	D#	E
F	Gb	A	Bb	Cb	Db	E	F
F#	G	A#	B	C	D	E#	F#
G	Ab	B	C	Db	Eb	F#	G
G#	A	C	C#	D	E	G	G#
A	Bb	C#	D	Eb	F	G#	A
Bb	Cb	D	Eb	Fb	Gb	A	Bb
B	C	D#	E	F	G	A#	B

Copyright 2013 by Kevin G. Pace
PaceMusicServices.com

East Indian Purvi

Considered an exotic scale, it could be called a Harmonic Major(b2, #4) scale.
It's like Harmonic Major with a lowered 2nd and raised 4th scale degree.
    For example: C East Indian Purvi = C-Db-E-F#-G-Ab-B-C
        (See #1 under ways to think about the scale)

Interesting or defining features:
Augmented 2nd between scale degrees 2 & 3, 6 & 7
Minor 2nds between scale degrees 1 & 2, 4 & 5, 5 & 6, 7 & 8

Chord that may be used with this scale: (example in C East Indian Purvi)
Major 7 (C-E-G-B)

Here are two ways to think about the East Indian Purvi scale:
1-Compare it to other scales
    For example:

C Major (Ionian)	C	D	E	F	G	A	B	C
C Harmonic Major	C	D	E	F	G	Ab	B	C
C East Indian Purvi	C	Db	E	F#	G	Ab	B	C

Could also be called Harmonic Major (2b, #4)

2-Think of the intervals between each note (m2=Minor 2nd, M2=Major 2nd, A2=Augmented 2nd)
For example: C East Indian Purvi   C   Db   E   F#   G   Ab   B   C
                                      m2   A2   M2   m2   m2   A2   m2

Here are the 12 East Indian Purvi scales:

Half-steps between notes:
    1-3-2-1-1-3-1

C	Db	E	F#	G	Ab	B	C
C#	D	E#	Fx	G#	A	B#	C#
D	Eb	F#	G#	A	Bb	C#	D
Eb	Fb	G	A	Bb	Cb	D	Eb
E	F	G#	A#	B	C	D#	E
F	Gb	A	B	C	Db	E	F
F#	G	A#	B#	C#	D	E#	F#
G	Ab	B	C#	D	Eb	F#	G
G#	A	B#	Cx	D#	E	Fx	G#
A	Bb	C#	D#	E	F	G#	A
Bb	Cb	D	E	F	Gb	A	Bb
B	C	D#	E#	F#	G	A#	B

Locrian #3

Considered an exotic scale, it is also called the Oriental scale.
It's like Locrian with a raised 3rd scale degree.
    For example: C Locrian #3 = C-Db-E-F-Gb-Ab-Bb-C
      (See #1 under ways to think about the scale)

Interesting or defining features:
Augmented 2nd between scale degrees 2 & 3
Minor 2nds between scale degrees 1 & 2, 3 & 4, 4 & 5

Chords that may be used with this scale: (example in C Locrian #3)
Dominant 7 (b5) (C-E-Gb-Bb)   Dominant 7 (b5, b9) (C-E-Gb-Bb-Db)
Dominant 7 (#5) (C-E-G#-Bb)   Dominant 7 (#5, b9) (C-E-G#-Bb-Db)

Here are two ways to think about the Locrian #3 scale:

1-Compare it to other scales
    For example:

C Natural Minor (Aeolian)	C	**D**	Eb	F	**G**	Ab	Bb	C
C Locrian	C	**Db**	**Eb**	F	**Gb**	Ab	Bb	C
C Locrian #3	C	Db	**E**	F	Gb	Ab	Bb	C

2-Think of the intervals between each note (m2=Minor 2nd, M2=Major 2nd, A2=Augmented 2nd)
    For example: C Locrian #3   C   Db   E   F   Gb   Ab   Bb   C
                                                            m2   A2   m2   m2   M2   M2   M2

Here are the 12 Locrian #3 scales:

Half-steps between notes:
    1-3-1-1-2-2-2

C	Db	E	F	Gb	Ab	Bb	C
C#	D	E#	F#	G	A	B	C#
D	Eb	F#	G	Ab	Bb	C	D
Eb	Fb	G	G#	A	Cb	Db	Eb
E	F	G#	A	Bb	C	D	E
F	Gb	A	Bb	Cb	Db	Eb	F
F#	G	A#	B	C	D	E	F#
G	Ab	B	C	Db	Eb	F	G
G#	A	B#	C#	D	E	F#	G#
A	Bb	C#	D	Eb	F	G	A
Bb	Cb	D	Eb	Fb	Gb	Ab	Bb
B	C	D#	E	F	G	A	B

(min 2nd between cols 1-2 and 3-4; Aug 2nd between cols 2-3; Whole tones between cols 4-5-6-7-8)

Copyright 2013 by Kevin G. Pace
PaceMusicServices.com

Synthetic Pentatonic Modes

Synthetic pentatonic modes are newly invented five-note scales. Some of the synthetic pentatonic modes are similar to the five previously discussed pentatonic modes (see pgs. 11-15). There are many, many possible combinations of five notes within an octave. I actually came up with 330 different possibilities. On the next few pages are some interesting possibilities. I have given some of these scales unique names which I believe describe these scale's unique characteristics.

Pg. 56
Major Pentatonic b6

Considered a synthetic pentatonic scale, it is an Altered Major Pentatonic Mode.
It's like the Major Pentatonic Mode (Mode 2) with a lowered 5th scale degree. The "b6" in the name is in reference to a major scale. For example, in C Major the flatted 6th scale degree is Ab.
    Example: C Major Pentatonic b6 = C-D-E-G-Ab-C (See #1 under ways to think about the scale).

Interesting or defining features:
Half step between scale degrees 4 & 5   3 half steps between scale degrees 3 & 4
4 half steps between scale degrees 5 & 1

Chords that may be used with this scale: (examples in C Major Pentatonic b6)
   Major(b6) (C-E-G-Ab)
   Aug Maj7 built on the altered note (a M3 below scale degree #1 (Ab-C-E-G). In other words, play
      this scale a M3 above the chord's root (in this example, C is a M3 above the chord's root).
   Minor-Major 7 built a P5 below scale degree 1 (F-Ab-C-E). In other words, play this scale a P4 below
      the chord's root (in this example, C is a P4 below the chord's root).
   Dominant 13(#11) chord built a M2 below the 1st note of this scale (Bb-D-F-Ab-C-E-G). In other words,
      play this scale a M2 above the chord's root (in this example, C is a M2 above the chord's root).
Note of interest: It is built on scale degrees 1, 2, 3, 5, and 6 of the Harmonic Major scale (see pg. 35)

Here are two ways to think about the Major Pentatonic b6 scale:
1-Compare it to other scales
      Two examples:

C Harmonic Major	C	D	E	F	G	Ab	B	C
C Major Pentatonic b6	C	D	E		G	Ab		C
C Major Pentatonic	C	D	E		G	A		C
C Major Pentatonic b6	C	D	E		G	Ab		C

2-Think of the intervals or half steps between each note
For example: C Major Pent b6   C   D   E   G   Ab   C
                                         2   2   3   1   4

Here are the 12 Major Pent b6 scales:

	C	D	E	G	Ab	C
	C#	D#	E#	G#	A	C#
	D	E	Gb	A	Bb	D
Half-steps between notes:	Eb	F	G	Bb	Cb	Eb
2-2-3-1-4	E	F#	G#	B	C	E
	F	G	A	C	Db	F
	F#	G#	A#	C#	D	F#
	G	A	B	D	Eb	G
	Ab	Bb	C	Eb	Fb	Ab
	A	B	C#	E	F	A
	Bb	C	D	F	Gb	Bb
	B	C#	D#	F#	G	B

Copyright 2013 by Kevin G. Pace
   PaceMusicServices.com

Major Pentatonic b3

Considered a synthetic pentatonic scale, it is an Altered Major Pentatonic Mode.
This is also called the Kumoi scale, an Asian pentatonic scale.
It's like the Major Pentatonic Mode (Mode 2) with a lowered 3rd scale degree.
    Example: C Major Pentatonic b3 = C-D-Eb-G-A-C (See #1 under ways to think about the scale).

Interesting or defining features:
Half step between scale degrees 2 & 3   3 half steps between scale degrees 5 & 1
4 half steps between scale degrees 3 & 4

Chords that may be used with this scale: (examples in C Major Pentatonic b3)
    Minor 6 (C-Eb-G-A)
    Augmented Dominant 7(#9) built a m2 below scale degree #1 (B-D#-G-A-D). In other words, play
        this scale a m2 above the chord's root (in this example, C is a m2 above the chord's root).

Here are two ways to think about the Major Pentatonic b3 scale:
1-Compare it to other scales
    Two examples:

C Major	C	D	E	F	G	A	B	C
C Major Pentatonic b3	C	D	Eb		G	A		C
C Major Pentatonic	C	D	E		G	A		C
C Major Pentatonic b3	C	D	Eb		G	A		C

2-Think of the intervals or half steps between each note

For example: C Major Pent b3	C	D	Eb	G	A	C
		2	1	4	2	3

Here are the 12 Major Pentatonic b3 scales:

	C	D	Eb	G	A	C
	C#	D#	E	G#	A#	C#
	D	E	F	A	B	D
Half-steps between notes:	Eb	F	Gb	Bb	C	Eb
2-1-4-2-3	E	F#	G	B	C#	E
	F	G	Ab	C	D	F
	F#	G#	A	C#	D#	F#
	G	A	Bb	D	E	G
	Ab	Bb	Cb	Eb	F	Ab
	A	B	C	E	F#	A
Copyright 2013 by Kevin G. Pace	Bb	C	Db	F	G	Bb
PaceMusicServices.com	B	C#	D	F#	G#	B

Minor 6 (add 4) Pentatonic

Considered a synthetic pentatonic scale, it is an Altered Minor Pentatonic Mode.
The notes of this scale are the same as a minor 6 chord with an added 4.
This is also called Minor Pentatonic (b5) - meaning the 5th note of Minor Pentatonic is lowered.
It's like the Minor Pentatonic Mode (Mode 1) with a lowered 5th scale degree.
    Example: C Minor 6 (add 4) Pentatonic = C-Eb-F-G-A-C (See #1 under ways to think about the scale).

Interesting or defining features:
3 half steps between scale degrees 1 & 2 and 5 & 1

Chords that may be used with this scale: (examples in C Minor 6 (add 4) Pentatonic)
  Minor 6 (C-Eb-G-A)   Dominant 7 (C-E-G-Bb)
  Minor 7 (C-Eb-G-Bb)
  Half-diminished 7 a minor 3rd below tonic (A-C-Eb-G)
Note of interest: It is built on scale degrees 1-3-4-5-6 of Melodic Minor (see pg. 21)

Here are two ways to think about the Minor 6 (add 4) Pentatonic scale:
1-Compare it to other scales
    Two examples:

C Melodic Minor	C	D	Eb	F	G	A	B	C
C Minor 6 (add 4) Pent	C		Eb	F	G	A		C
C Minor Pentatonic	C		Eb	F	G		Bb	C
C Minor 6 (add 4) Pent	C		Eb	F	G	A		C

2-Think of the intervals or half steps between each note
For example: C Minor 6 (add 4) Pent   C   Eb   F   G   A   C
                                                        3   2   2   2   3

Here are the 12 Minor 6 (add 4) Pentatonic Scales:

Half-steps between notes:
3-2-2-2-3

C	Eb	F	G	A	C
C#	E	F#	G#	A#	C#
D	F	G	A	B	D
Eb	Gb	Ab	Bb	C	Eb
E	G	A	B	C#	E
F	Ab	Bb	C	D	F
F#	A	B	C#	D#	F#
G	Bb	C	D	E	G
Ab	Cb	Db	Eb	F	Ab
A	C	D	E	F#	A
Bb	Db	Eb	F	G	Bb
B	D	E	F#	G#	B

Copyright 2013 by Kevin G. Pace
PaceMusicServices.com

Half-diminished (add 4) Pentatonic

Considered a synthetic pentatonic scale, it is an Altered Minor Pentatonic Mode.
The notes of this scale are the same as a half-diminished 7 chord with an added 4.
This is also called Minor Pentatonic (b4) - meaning the 4th note of Minor Pentatonic is lowered.
It's like the Minor Pentatonic Mode (Mode 1) with a lowered 4th scale degree.
    Example: C Half-dim (add 4) Pent = C-Eb-F-Gb-Bb-C (See #1 under ways to think about the scale).

Interesting or defining features:
3 half steps between scale degrees 1 & 2   Half step between scale degrees 3 & 4
4 half steps between scale degrees 4 & 5

Chords that may be used with this scale: (examples in C Half-diminished (add 4) Pentatonic)
    Half-diminished 7 (C-Eb-Gb-Bb)
    Minor 6 built on 2nd note of scale (Eb-Gb-Bb-C)
Note of interest: It is built on scale degrees 1-3-4-5-7 of the Locrian Scale

Here are two ways to think about the Half-diminished (add 4) Pentatonic scale:
1-Compare it to other scales
    Two examples:

C Locrian	C	Db	Eb	F	Gb	Ab	Bb	C
C Half-dim (add 4) Pent	C		Eb	F	Gb		Bb	C
C Minor Pentatonic	C		Eb	F	G		Bb	C
C Half-dim (add 4) Pent	C		Eb	F	Gb		Bb	C

2-Think of the intervals or half steps between each note
For example: C Half-dim (add 4) Pent   C   Eb   F   Gb   Bb   C
                                              3   2   1   4   2

Here are the 12 Half-diminished (add 4) Pentatonic Scales:

Half-steps between notes:
    3-2-1-4-2

C	Eb	F	Gb	Bb	C
C#	E	F#	G	B	C#
D	F	G	Ab	C	D
D#	F#	G#	A	C#	D#
E	G	A	Bb	D	E
F	Ab	Bb	Cb	Eb	F
F#	A	B	C	E	F#
G	Bb	C	Db	F	G
G#	B	C#	D	F#	G#
A	C	D	Eb	G	A
Bb	Db	Eb	Fb	Ab	Bb
B	D	E	F	A	B

Copyright 2013 by Kevin G. Pace
    PaceMusicServices.com

Lydian Augmented Major 7 Pentatonic

A synthetic pentatonic scale with a Lydian Augmented Major 7 sound.
Notice how the notes of this scale are the same as those in the Lydian Augmented scale.
   Example: C Lydian Augmented Major 7 Pentatonic = C-E-F#-G#-B-C
It's like a Major 7 chord with the 5 being replaced by a #4 and a #5.
   (See #1 under ways to think about the scale)

Interesting or defining features:
4 half steps between scale degrees 1 & 2   Half step between scale degrees 5 & 1
3 half steps between scale degrees 4 & 5

Chord that may be used with this scale: (examples in C Lydian Augmented Major 7 Pentatonic)
   Augmented Major 7 (C-E-G#-B)

Note of interest: It is built on scale degrees 1-3-4-5-7 of the Lydian Augmented Scale (see pg 23)

Here are two ways to think about the Lydian Augmented Major 7 Pentatonic scale:
1-Compare it to other scales
   Two examples:

C Lydian Augmented	C	D	E	F#	G#	A	B	C
C Lydian Aug Major 7 Pent	C		E	F#	G#		B	C
C Major (Ionian)	C	D	E	F	G	A	B	C
C Lydian Aug Major 7 Pent	C		E	F#	G#		B	C

2-Think of the intervals or half steps between each note
For example: C Lydian Aug Major Pent   C   E   F#   G#   B   C
                                       4   2   2   3   1

Here are the 12 Lydian Augmented Major 7 Pentatonic Scales:

Half-steps between notes:
   4-2-2-3-1

C	E	F#	G#	B	C
Db	F	G	A	C	Db
D	F#	G#	A#	C#	D
Eb	G	A	B	D	Eb
E	G#	A#	C	D#	E
F	A	B	Db	E	F
Gb	Bb	C	D	F	Gb
G	B	C#	D#	F#	G
Ab	C	D	E	G	Ab
A	C#	D#	F	G#	A
Bb	D	E	Gb	A	Bb
B	D#	F	G	A#	B

Copyright 2013 by Kevin G. Pace
PaceMusicServices.com

Minor Lydian Augmented Pentatonic

A synthetic pentatonic scale with a minor Lydian Augmented sound.
Notice how the notes of this scale are similar to those in the Lydian Augmented scale.
  Example: C Minor Lydian Augmented Pentatonic = C-Eb-F#-G#-B-C
It's like a Minor Major 7 chord with the 5 being replaced by a #4 and a #5.
  (See #1 under ways to think about the scale)

Interesting or defining features:
Half step between scale degrees 5 & 1
3 half steps between scale degrees 1 & 2, 2 & 3, and 4 & 5.

Chords that may be used with this scale: (examples in C Minor Lydian Augmented Pentatonic)
  Dominant 7 chord built on 4th note of scale (Ab-C-Eb-Gb). In other words, play this scale a
    Major 3rd above the root of the chord.
  Dominant 7(#9) chord built on 4th note of scale (Ab-C-Eb-Gb-B).
  Minor Major 7(#5) (C-Eb-G#-B)

Here are two ways to think about the Minor Lydian Augmented Pentatonic scale:
1-Compare it to other scales

C Lydian Augmented	C	D	E	F#	G#	A	B	C
C Minor Lydian Aug Pent	C		Eb	F#	G#		B	C

2-Think of the intervals or half steps between each note
For example: C Minor Lydian Aug Pent   C   Eb   F#   G#   B   C
                                          3   3   2   3   1

Here are the 12 Minor Lydian Augmented Pentatonic Scales:

Half-steps between notes:
     3-3-2-3-1

C	Eb	F#	G#	B	C
Db	E	G	A	C	Db
D	F	G#	A#	C#	D
Eb	F#	A	B	D	Eb
E	G	A#	C	D#	E
F	Ab	B	Db	E	F
Gb	A	C	D	F	Gb
G	A#	C#	D#	F#	G
Ab	B	D	E	G	Ab
A	C	D#	F	G#	A
Bb	Db	E	Gb	A	Bb
B	D	F	G	A#	B

Copyright 2013 by Kevin G. Pace
PaceMusicServices.com

Lydian Augmented (add 9) Pentatonic

A synthetic pentatonic scale with a Lydian Augmented sound.
Notice how the notes of this scale are similar to those in the Lydian Augmented scale.
   Example: C Lydian Augmented (add 9) Pentatonic = C-D-F#-G#-B-C
The #4 and #5 give it a Lydian Augmented feel, the 2 gives it an add 9 feel.
It is the same as a Lydian Augmented scale using only scale degrees 1-2-4-5-7.
     (see #1 under ways to think of this scale)

Interesting or defining features:
Half step between scale degrees 5 & 1.   4 half steps between scale degrees 2 & 3.
3 half steps between scale degrees 4 & 5.

Chords that may be used with this scale: (examples in C Lydian Augmented (add 9) Pentatonic)
   Augmented Major 7 (C-E-G#-B)
   Lydian Augmented Major 7 (C-F#-G#-B)

Here are two ways to think about the Lydian Augmented (add 9) Pentatonic scale:
1-Compare it to other scales

C Lydian Augmented	C	D	E	F#	G#	A	B	C
C Lydian Aug (add 9) Pent	C	D		F#	G#		B	C
C Major (Ionian)	C	D	E	F	G	A	B	C
C Lydian Aug (add 9) Pent	C	D		F#	G#		B	C

2-Think of the intervals or half steps between each note
For example: C Lydian Aug (add 9) Pent   C   D   F#   G#   B   C
                                               2   4   2   3   1

Here are the 12 Lydian Augmented (add 9) Pentatonic Scales:

	C	D	F#	G#	B	C
	Db	Eb	G	A	C	Db
	D	E	G#	A#	C#	D
Half-steps between notes:	Eb	F	A	B	D	Eb
2-4-2-3-1	E	F#	A#	C	D#	E
	F	G	B	Db	E	F
	Gb	Ab	C	D	F	Gb
	G	A	C#	D#	F#	G
	Ab	Bb	D	E	G	Ab
	A	B	D#	F	G#	A
	Bb	C	E	Gb	A	Bb
	B	C#	F	G	A#	B

Copyright 2013 by Kevin G. Pace
PaceMusicServices.com

Half-diminished 9 Pentatonic

A synthetic pentatonic scale with a half-diminished 7 sound.
Notice how the notes of this scale outline a half-diminished 7 chord with an added 9.
    Example: C Half-diminished 9 Pentatonic = C-D-Eb-Gb-Bb-C
It is the same as a Locrian #2 scale using only scale degrees 1-2-3-5-7.
    (see #1 under ways to think of this scale)

Interesting or defining features:

Half step between scale degrees 2 & 3   4 half steps between scale degrees 4 & 5
3 half steps between scale degrees 3 & 4

Chords that may be used with this scale: (examples in C Half-diminished 9 Pentatonic)

    Half-diminished 9 (C-Eb-Gb-Bb-D)   Minor 6 starting on 3rd scale degree (Eb-Gb-Bb-C). In other words,
    Half-diminished 7 (C-Eb-Gb-Bb)   play the scale starting a minor 3rd below the root of the chord.

Here are two ways to think about the Half-diminished 9 Pentatonic scale:

1-Compare it to other scales
    Two examples:

C Locrian #2	C	D	Eb	F	Gb	Ab	Bb	C
C Half-dim 9 Pent	C	D	Eb		Gb		Bb	C
C Locrian	C	Db	Eb	F	Gb	Ab	Bb	C
C Half-dim 9 Pent	C	D	Eb		Gb		Bb	C

2-Think of the intervals or half steps between each note
For example: C Half-dim 9 Pent   C   D   Eb   Gb   Bb   C
                                                              2   1   3   4   2

Here are the 12 Half-diminished 9 Pentatonic Scales:

Half-steps between notes:
    2-1-3-4-2

C	D	Eb	Gb	Bb	C
C#	D#	E	G	B	C#
D	E	F	Ab	C	D
Eb	F	Gb	A	Db	Eb
E	F#	G	A#	D	E
F	G	Ab	B	Eb	F
F#	G#	A	C	E	F#
G	A	Bb	Db	F	G
Ab	Bb	Cb	D	F#	Ab
A	B	C	Eb	G	A
Bb	C	Db	E	Ab	Bb
B	C#	D	F	A	B

Half-diminished b13 Pentatonic

A synthetic pentatonic scale with a half-diminished 7 sound.
Notice how the notes of this scale outline a half-diminished 7 chord with an added b13 (b6).
    Example: C Half-diminished b13 Pentatonic = C-Eb-Gb-Ab-Bb-C
It is the same as the Altered Scale using only scale degrees 1-3-5-6-7.
    (see #1 under ways to think of this scale)

Interesting or defining features:
3 half steps between scale degrees 1 & 2 and 2 & 3. The rest of the scale is whole steps.

Chords that may be used with this scale: (examples in C Half-diminished b13 Pentatonic)
    Dominant 7 starting on 4th scale degree (Ab-C-Eb-Gb). (Play scale starting a major 3rd above chord's root).
    Dominant 9 starting on 4th scale degree (Ab-C-Eb-Gb-Bb)
    Half-diminished 7 (C-Eb-Gb-Bb)

Here are two ways to think about the Half-diminished b13 Pentatonic scale:
1-Compare it to other scales
    Two examples:

C Altered Scale	C	Db	Eb	Fb	Gb	Ab	Bb	C
C Half-dim b13 Pent	C		Eb		Gb	Ab	Bb	C
C Locrian	C	Db	Eb	F	Gb	Ab	Bb	C
C Half-dim b13 Pent	C		Eb		Gb	Ab	Bb	C

2-Think of the intervals or half steps between each note
For example: C Half-dim b13 Pent   C   Eb   Gb   Ab   Bb   C
                                              3   3   2   2   2

Here are the 12 Half-diminished b13 Pentatonic Scales:

Half-steps between notes:
3-3-2-2-2

C	Eb	Gb	Ab	Bb	C
C#	E	G	A	B	C#
D	F	Ab	Bb	C	D
Eb	Gb	A	B	Db	Eb
E	G	Bb	C	D	E
F	Ab	B	Db	Eb	F
F#	A	C	D	E	F#
G	Bb	Db	Eb	F	G
Ab	B	D	E	Gb	Ab
A	C	Eb	F	G	A
Bb	Db	E	Gb	Ab	Bb
B	D	F	G	A	B

Copyright 2013 by Kevin G. Pace
PaceMusicServices.com

Diminished 9 Pentatonic

A synthetic pentatonic scale with a fully diminished 7 sound.
Notice how the notes of this scale outline a fully diminished 7 chord with an added 9.
   Example: C Diminished 9 Pentatonic = C-D-Eb-Gb-A-C
It is the same as the Dorian #4 Scale using only scale degrees 1-2-3-4-6.
   (see #1 under ways to think of this scale)

Interesting or defining features:
3 half steps between scale degrees 3 & 4 and 4 & 5 and 5 & 1.
Half step between scale degrees 2 & 3.

Chords that may be used with this scale: (examples in C Diminished 9 Pentatonic)
   Dominant 7 starting on 2nd scale degree (D-F#-A-C). (Play scale starting a major 2nd below chord's root).
   Dominant 7(b9) starting on 2nd scale degree (D-F#-A-C-Eb).
   Diminished 7 (C-Eb-Gb-Bbb). Note: Bbb = A.

Here are two ways to think about the Diminished 9 Pentatonic scale:
1-Compare it to other scales
   Two examples:

C Dorian #4 Scale	C	D	Eb	F#	G	A	Bb	C
C Diminished 9 Pent	C	D	Eb	F#		A		C
C Dorian	C	D	Eb	**F**	G	A	Bb	C
C Diminished 9 Pent	C	D	Eb	**F#**		A		C

2-Think of the intervals or half steps between each note
For example: C Diminished 9 Pent   C   D   Eb   Gb   A   C
                                        2   1   3   3   3

Here are the 12 Diminished 9 Pentatonic Scales:

C	D	Eb	Gb	A	C
C#	D#	E	G	A#	C#
D	E	F	Ab	B	D
Eb	F	Gb	A	C	Eb
E	F#	G	Bb	Db	E
F	G	Ab	B	D	F
F#	G#	A	C	D#	F#
G	A	Bb	Db	E	G
G#	A#	B	D	F	G#
A	B	C	Eb	F#	A
Bb	C	Db	E	G	Bb
B	C#	D	F	G#	B

Half-steps between notes: 2-1-3-3-3

Diminished (add 11) Pentatonic

A synthetic pentatonic scale with a fully diminished 7 sound.
Notice how the notes of this scale outline a fully diminished 7 chord with an added 11 (or 4).
    Example: C Diminished (add 11) Pentatonic = C-Eb-F-Gb-A-C
It is the same as the Dorian b5 Scale using only scale degrees 1-3-4-5-6.
    (see #1 under ways to think of this scale)

Interesting or defining features:
3 half steps between scale degrees 1 & 2, 4 & 5, and 5 & 1.
Half step between scale degrees 3 & 4.

Chords that may be used with this scale: (examples in C Diminished (add 11) Pentatonic)
    Dominant 7 starting on 3rd scale degree (F-A-C-Eb). (Play scale starting a Perfect 5 above chord's root).
    Dominant 7(b9) starting on 3rd scale degree (F-A-C-Eb-Gb).
    Diminished 7 (C-Eb-Gb-Bbb). Note: Bbb = A.

Here are two ways to think about the Diminished (add 11) Pentatonic scale:
1-Compare it to other scales
    Two examples:

C Dorian b5 Scale	C	D	Eb	F	Gb	A	Bb	C
C Dim (add 11) Pent	C		Eb	F	Gb	A		C
C Dorian	C	D	Eb	F	**G**	A	Bb	C
C Dim (add 11) Pent	C		Eb	F	**Gb**	A		C

2-Think of the intervals or half steps between each note
For example: C Dim (add 11) Pent   C   Eb   F   Gb   A   C
                                          3   2   1   3   3

Here are the 12 Diminished (add 11) Pentatonic Scales:

Half-steps between notes:
    3-2-1-3-3

C	Eb	F	Gb	A	C
C#	E	F#	G	A#	C#
D	F	G	Ab	B	D
D#	F#	G#	A	C	D#
E	G	A	Bb	Db	E
F	Ab	Bb	B	D	F
F#	A	B	C	D#	F#
G	Bb	C	Db	E	G
G#	B	C#	D	F	G#
A	C	D	Eb	Gb	A
Bb	Db	Eb	E	G	Bb
B	D	E	F	G#	B

Copyright 2013 by Kevin G. Pace
PaceMusicServices.com

Diminished (#5) Pentatonic

A synthetic pentatonic scale with a fully diminished 7 sound.
Notice how the notes of this scale outline a fully diminished 7 chord with an added #5.
   Example: C Diminished (#5) Pentatonic = C-Eb-F#-G#-A-C
It is the same as the Altered b7 Scale using only scale degrees 1-3-5-6-7.
   (see #1 under ways to think of this scale)

Interesting or defining features:
3 half steps between scale degrees 1 & 2, 2 & 3, and 5 & 1.
Half step between scale degrees 4 & 5.

Chords that may be used with this scale: (examples in C Diminished (#5) Pentatonic)
   Dominant 7 starting on 4th scale degree (Ab-C-Eb-Gb). (Play scale starting a Major 3rd above chord's root).
   Dominant 7(b9) starting on 4th scale degree (Ab-C-Eb-Gb-Bbb).
   Diminished 7 (C-Eb-Gb-Bbb). Note: Bbb = A.

Here are two ways to think about the Diminished (#5) Pentatonic scale:
1-Compare it to other scales
   Two examples:

C Altered b7 Scale	C	Db	Eb	Fb	Gb	Ab	Bbb	C
C Dim (#5) Pent	C		Eb		F#	G#	A	C
C Altered Scale	C	Db	Eb	Fb	Gb	Ab	**Bb**	C
C Dim (#5) Pent	C		Eb		F#	G#	**A**	C

2-Think of the intervals or half steps between each note
For example: C Dim (#5) Pentatonic   C   Eb   F#   G#   A   C
                                        3   3   2   1   3

Here are the 12 Diminished (#5) Pentatonic Scales:

	C	Eb	F#	G#	A	C
	C#	E	G	A	Bb	C#
	D	F	G#	A#	B	D
Half-steps between notes:	D#	F#	A	B	C	D#
3-3-2-1-3	E	G	Bb	C	Db	E
	F	G#	B	C#	D	F
	Gb	A	C	D	Eb	Gb
	G	A#	C#	D#	E	G
	G#	B	D	E	F	G#
	A	C	Eb	F	Gb	A
	Bb	Db	E	F#	G	Bb
	B	D	F	G	Ab	B

Copyright 2013 by Kevin G. Pace
PaceMusicServices.com

Pg. 68
Diminished Major 7 Pentatonic

A synthetic pentatonic scale with a fully diminished Major 7 sound.
Notice how the notes of this scale outline a fully diminished 7 chord with an added Major 7.
   Example: C Diminished Major 7 Pentatonic = C-Eb-F#-A-B-C
It is the same as the Lydian b3 Scale using only scale degrees 1-3-4-6-7.
     (see #1 under ways to think of this scale)

Interesting or defining features:
3 half steps between scale degrees 1 & 2, 2 & 3, and 3 & 4.
Half step between scale degrees 5 & 1.

Chords that may be used with this scale: (examples in C Diminished Major 7 Pentatonic)
   Dominant 7 starting on 5th scale degree (B-D#-F#-A). (Play scale starting a half step above chord's root).
   Dominant 7(b9) starting on 5th scale degree (B-D#-F#-A-C).
   Fully Diminished 7 (C-Eb-Gb-Bbb). Note: Bbb = A.
   Diminished Major 7 (C-Eb-Gb-B).

Here are two ways to think about the Diminished Major 7 Pentatonic scale:
1-Compare it to other scales
   Two examples:

C Lydian b3 Scale	C	D	Eb	F#	G	A	B	C
C Dim Major 7 Pent	C		Eb	F#		A	B	C
C Lydian Scale	C	D	**E**	F#	G	A	B	C
C Dim Major 7 Pent	C		**Eb**	F#		A	B	C

2-Think of the intervals or half steps between each note
For example: C Dim Major 7 Pentatonic   C   Eb   F#   A   B   C
                                                                3   3   3   2   1

Here are the 12 Diminished Major 7 Pentatonic Scales:

	C	Eb	F#	A	B	C
	Db	E	G	Bb	C	Db
	D	F	G#	B	C#	D
Half-steps between notes:	Eb	F#	A	C	D	Eb
3-3-3-2-1	E	G	A#	C#	D#	E
	F	G#	B	D	E	F
	Gb	A	C	Eb	F	Gb
	G	A#	C#	E	F#	G
	Ab	B	D	F	G	Ab
	A	C	Eb	Gb	Ab	A
	Bb	Db	E	G	A	Bb
	B	D	F	G#	A#	B

Copyright 2013 by Kevin G. Pace
   PaceMusicServices.com

Dominant 9 Pentatonic

A synthetic pentatonic scale with a Dominant 7 sound.
Notice how the notes of this scale outline a Dominant 7 chord with an added Major 9.
   Example: C Dominant 9 Pentatonic = C-D-E-G-Bb-C
It is the same as the Mixolydian Scale using only scale degrees 1-2-3-5-7.
    (see #1 under ways to think of this scale)

Interesting or defining features:
3 half steps between scale degrees 3 & 4 and 4 & 5.

Chords that may be used with this scale: (examples in C Dominant 9 Pentatonic)
   Dominant 7 (C-E-G-Bb)
   Dominant 9 (C-E-G-Bb-D)

Here are two ways to think about the Dominant 9 Pentatonic scale:

1-Compare it to other scales
   Two examples:

C Mixolydian Scale	C	D	E	F	G	A	Bb	C
C Dom 9 Pent	C	D	E		G		Bb	C
C Major Scale (Ionian)	C	D	E	F	G	A	**B**	C
C Dom 9 Pent	C	D	E		G		**Bb**	C

2-Think of the intervals or half steps between each note
For example: C Dominant 9 Pent   C   D   E   G   Bb   C
                                                2   2   3   3   2

Here are the 12 Dominant 9 Pentatonic Scales:

Half-steps between notes:
   2-2-3-3-2

C	D	E	G	Bb	C
Db	Eb	F	Ab	B	Db
D	E	F#	A	C	D
Eb	F	G	Bb	Db	Eb
E	F#	G#	B	D	E
F	G	A	C	Eb	F
F#	G#	A#	C#	E	F#
G	A	B	D	F	G
Ab	Bb	C	Eb	Gb	Ab
A	B	C#	E	G	A
Bb	C	D	F	Ab	Bb
B	C#	D#	F#	A	B

Copyright 2013 by Kevin G. Pace
PaceMusicServices.com

Pelog Pentatonic

An Asian Pentatonic scale
The notes of this scale are the same as scale degrees 1, 2, 3, 5, & 6 of the Phrygian mode.
    Example: C Pelog Pentatonic = C-Db-Eb-G-Ab-C
      (see #1 under ways to think of this scale)

Interesting or defining features:
Half steps between scale degrees 1 & 2 and 4 & 5
4 half steps between scale degrees 3 & 4 and 5 & 1

Chords that may be used with this scale: (examples in C Pelog Pentatonic)
  Minor b6 (C-Eb-G-Ab)
  Dominant 7 built a M3 below the tonic (Ab-C-Eb-Gb). In other words, play the scale a M3 above chord's root.
  Major 7 built a M3 below the tonic (Ab-C-Eb-G). In other words, play the scale a M3 above chord's root.

Here are two ways to think about the Pelog Pentatonic scale:
1-Compare it to other scales

	C	Db	Eb	F	G	Ab	Bb	C
C Phrygian Scale	C	Db	Eb	F	G	Ab	Bb	C
C Pelog Pentatonic	C	Db	Eb		G	Ab		C

2-Think of the intervals or half steps between each note
For example: C Pelog Pent

	C	Db	Eb	G	Ab	C
	1	2	4	1	4	

Here are the 12 Pelog Pentatonic Scales:

Half-steps between notes:
1-2-4-1-4

C	Db	Eb	G	Ab	C
Db	D	E	Ab	A	Db
D	Eb	F	A	Bb	D
Eb	E	Gb	Bb	B	Eb
E	F	G	B	C	E
F	Gb	Ab	C	Db	F
F#	G	A	C#	D	F#
G	Ab	Bb	D	Eb	G
Ab	A	B	D#	E	Ab
A	Bb	C	E	F	A
Bb	B	C#	F	Gb	Bb
B	C	D	F#	G	B

Copyright 2013 by Kevin G. Pace
PaceMusicServices.com

Hirajoshi Pentatonic

An Asian Pentatonic scale
The notes of this scale are the same as scale degrees 1, 2, 3, 5, & 6 of the Aeolian mode.
    Example: C Hirajoshi Pentatonic = C-D-Eb-G-Ab-C
       (see #1 under ways to think of this scale)

Interesting or defining features:
Half steps between scale degrees 2 & 3 and 4 & 5
4 half steps between scale degrees 3 & 4 and 5 & 1

Chords that may be used with this scale: (examples in C Hirajoshi Pentatonic)
    Minor b6 (C-Eb-G-Ab)
    Minor (add 9) (C-D-Eb-G)
    Major 7 built a M3 below the tonic (Ab-C-Eb-G).

Here are two ways to think about the Hirajoshi Pentatonic scale:
1-Compare it to other scales

C Aeolian Scale	C	D	Eb	F	G	Ab	Bb	C
C Hirajoshi Pentatonic	C	D	Eb		G	Ab		C

2-Think of the intervals or half steps between each note
For example: C Hirajoshi Pent

C	D	Eb	G	Ab	C
	2	1	4	1	4

Here are the 12 Hirajoshi Pentatonic Scales:

Half-steps between notes:
2-1-4-1-4

C	D	Eb	G	Ab	C
Db	Eb	E	Ab	A	Db
D	E	F	A	Bb	D
Eb	F	Gb	Bb	B	Eb
E	F#	G	B	C	E
F	G	Ab	C	Db	F
F#	G#	A	C#	D	F#
G	A	Bb	D	Eb	G
Ab	Bb	B	D#	E	Ab
A	B	C	E	F	A
Bb	C	Db	F	Gb	Bb
B	C#	D	F#	G	B

Copyright 2013 by Kevin G. Pace
PaceMusicServices.com

Other Possible Synthetic Scales

Adding or altering a note (or multiple notes) to an existing scale can give you interesting results.

There are numerous options here.

On the next few pages are some possibilities, just to give you an idea.

Some ideas to consider:

Synthetic scales are great for composers. By "inventing" a new scale with the addition or alteration of one or two changed notes, you can get some very interesting and unique sounds. You could try basing a whole composition on one of these synthetic scales.

Copyright 2013 by Kevin G. Pace
PaceMusicServices.com

Pg. 73
Ionian b2 Scale

The Ionian b2 Mode is a major scale with a lowered 2nd scale degree.

Interesting or defining features:
Half steps between scale degrees 1 & 2, 3 & 4, and 7 & 8.   3 half steps between scale degrees 2 & 3.

Chords that may be used with this scale: (examples in C Ionian b2)
Major triad (C-E-G)
Major 7 (C-E-G-B)
Major 7(b9) (C-E-G-B-Db)

Here are two ways to think about the Ionian b2 scale:
1-Compare it to another scale
   For example:
      C Ionian (Major)   C   **D**   E   F   G   A   B   C
      C Ionian b2   C   **Db**   E   F   G   A   B   C

2-Think of half-steps between notes
   For example: C   Db   E   F   G   A   B   C
                               1   3   1   2   2   2   1

Here are the 12 Ionian b2 scales:

		min 3rd					
	min 2nd		min 2nd			min 2nd	
C	Db	E	F	G	A	B	C
Db	Ebb	F	Gb	Ab	Bb	C	Db
D	Eb	F#	G	A	B	C#	D
Eb	Fb	G	Ab	Bb	C	D	Eb
E	F	G#	A	B	C#	D#	E
F	Gb	A	Bb	C	D	E	F
F#	G	A#	B	C#	D#	E#	F#
G	Ab	B	C	D	E	F#	G
Ab	Bbb	C	Db	Eb	F	G	Ab
A	Bb	C#	D	E	F#	G#	A
Bb	Cb	D	Eb	F	G	A	Bb
B	C	D#	E	F#	G#	A#	B

Half-steps between notes:
   1-3-1-2-2-2-1

Copyright 2013 by Kevin G. Pace
PaceMusicServices.com

Pg. 74

Aeolian b4

The Aeolian b4 scale is like the natural minor scale (Aeolian) with a lowered 4th scale degree.

Example: C   D   Eb   Fb   G   Ab   Bb   C
                          (E)

Interesting or defining features:
Minor 2nds (half steps) between scale degrees 2 & 3, 3 & 4, and 5 & 6.
3 half steps between scale degrees 4 & 5.

Chords that may be used with this scale: (examples in C Aeolian b4)
Dominant 7 (C-E-G-Bb)
Minor 7 (C-Eb-G-Bb)
Minor 9(b11/b13) (C-Eb-G-Bb-D-Fb-Ab)
   One possible way to play this chord is to play a low C, with pedal on, then play Bb-Eb-Fb-Ab
   (This is an unconventional chord, which is one of the beauties of synthetic scales).

or play this: [Bb7(b5) / C minor triad]   [Dom 7(b5) Maj 2 below root / Root minor triad]

Here are two ways to think about the Aeolian b4 mode:
1-Compare it to another scale
   For example: A Aeolian   A   B   C   D   E   F   G   A
                 A Aeolian b4   A   B   C   Db   E   F   G   A

2-Think of the intervals or half steps between each note
   For example:
                 A Aeolian b4   A   B   C   Db   E   F   G   A
                                 2   1   1   3   1   2   2

			half-step		half-step		
		half-step					
Here are the 12 Aeolian b4 scales:	C	D	Eb	Fb	G	Ab	Bb	C
	C#	D#	E	F	G#	A	B	C#
Half-steps between notes:	D	E	F	Gb	A	Bb	C	D
2-1-1-3-1-2-2	Eb	F	Gb	Abb	Bb	Cb	Db	Eb
	E	F#	G	Ab	B	C	D	E
	F	G	Ab	Bbb	C	Db	Eb	F
	F#	G#	A	Bb	C#	D	E	F#
	G	A	Bb	Cb	D	Eb	F	G
	G#	A#	B	C	D#	E	F#	G#
	A	B	C	Db	E	F	G	A
	Bb	C	Db	Ebb	F	Gb	Ab	Bb
	B	C#	D	Eb	F#	G	A	B

3 half-steps

Copyright 2013 by Kevin G. Pace
PaceMusicServices.com

Bebop Dorian

It is a Dorian Scale with an added passing tone between the 3rd & 4th scale degrees.

Example: D E F F# (Gb) G A B C D

Interesting or defining features:
Minor 2nds (half-steps) between scale degrees 2 & 3, 3 & 4, 4 & 5, and 7 & 8.

Chords that may be used with this scale: (examples in D Bebop Dorian)
Minor 7 (D-F-A-C)
Dominant 7 (D-F#-A-C)

Here are two ways to think about the Bebop Dorian mode:
1-Compare it to another scale.
   For example:
   D Dorian: D E F   G A B C D
   D Bebop Dorian: D E F **F#** G A B C D

2-Think of the intervals or half-steps between each scale degree.
   For example:
   D Bebop Dorian: D E F F# G A B C D
                    2 1 1 1 2 2 1 2

Here are the 12 Bebop Dorian scales:

Half-steps between notes:
2-1-1-1-2-2-1-2

		min 2nd				min 2nd	
C	D	Eb	E	F	G	A	Bb	C
C#	D#	E	F	F#	G#	A#	B	C#
D	E	F	F#	G	A	B	C	D
Eb	F	Gb	G	Ab	Bb	C	Db	Eb
E	F#	G	G#	A	B	C#	D	E
F	G	Ab	A	Bb	C	D	Eb	F
F#	G#	A	Bb	B	C#	D#	E	F#
G	A	Bb	B	C	D	E	F	G
G#	A#	B	C	C#	D#	E#	F#	G#
A	B	C	Db	D	E	F#	G	A
Bb	C	Db	D	Eb	F	G	Ab	Bb
B	C#	D	Eb	E	F#	G#	A	B
		min 2nd					
			min 2nd				

Pg. 76
Lydian Dominant b2

A synthetic scale
Similar to the 4th mode of Melodic Minor with a flatted 2nd scale degree.
    Example: C Lydian Dominant b2 = C-Db-E-F#-G-A-Bb-C

Interesting or defining features:
Minor 2nds between scale degrees 1 & 2, 4 & 5, 6 & 7.

Chords that may be used with this scale: (examples in C Lydian Dominant b2)
Dominant 7 (C-E-G-Bb)　　　　Major 6 (C-E-G-A)　　　　Dominant 7(b5) (C-E-Gb-Bb)

Dominant 13(b9/#11) (C-E-G-Bb-Db-F#-A). Or think this way:　[F# Minor Triad 2nd inversion / C Dominant 7]

[2nd inv min triad, low note m3 above 7th / Root Dom 7]

(See chords for Lydian Dominant scale as well)

Here are two ways to think about the Lydian Dominant b2 scale:
1-Compare it to other scales
    For example:

C Major:	C	D	E	F	G	A	**B**	C
C Mixolydian:	C	D	E	**F**	G	A	**Bb**	C
C Lydian Dominant:	C	**D**	E	**F#**	G	A	**Bb**	C
C Lydian Dominant b2:	C	**Db**	E	**F#**	G	A	**Bb**	C

Lydian Dominant b2 is a Major scale with altered scale degrees 2, 4, & 7.

2-Think of the intervals or half-steps between each scale degree.
    For example:

C Lydian Dominant b2:	C	Db	E	F#	G	A	Bb	C
	1	3	2	1	2	1	2	

Here are the 12 Lydian Dominant b2 scales:

Half-steps between notes:
1-3-2-1-2-1-2

C	Db	E	F#	G	A	Bb	C
Db	Ebb	F	G	Ab	Bb	Cb	Db
D	Eb	F#	G#	A	B	C	D
Eb	Fb	G	A	Bb	C	Db	Eb
E	F	G#	A#	B	C#	D	E
F	Gb	A	B	C	D	Eb	F
F#	G	A#	B#	C#	D#	E	F#
G	Ab	B	C#	D	E	F	G
Ab	Bbb	C	D	Eb	F	Gb	Ab
A	Bb	C#	D#	E	F#	G	A
Bb	Cb	D	E	F	G	Ab	Bb
B	C	D#	E#	F#	G#	A	B

Copyright 2013 by Kevin G. Pace
PaceMusicServices.com

Other Interesting Scales

The possibilities to form different scales are practically endless. Here are a few more ideas.

1-Try inverting the exotic scales

2-Various 6 note scales

3-Other 8 note scales

4-Nine note scales

5-Ten note scales

6-Other Bebop scales:

    Bebop Melodic Minor (put a chromatic passing tone between scale degrees 5 & 6)

    Bebop Harmonic Minor (put a b7 between scale degrees 6 & 7)

See examples on the next five pages.

Arabian Major 3rd Mode

This is one example of an inverted exotic scale (Arabian Major in its 3rd mode).
It's like 3 notes of a chromatic scale followed by a whole tone scale.

	Example:	C	Db	Ebb	Fb	Gb	Ab	Bb	C
				(D)	(E)				

Interesting or defining features:
Half-steps from scale degrees 1 through 3.   Whole tones from scale degrees 3 through 8.
It's like a whole tone scale with an added b9.

Chords that may be used with this scale: (examples in C Arabian Major Mode 3)
Dominant 7(b5) in first inversion (e.g. C7(b5(/E) (E-Gb-Bb-C)
Minor-Major 7 built on 2nd scale degree (C#-E-G#-B#). Play scale starting a minor 2nd below chord's root.
Dominant 7 (C-E-G-Bb)
Dominant 7 chord built on 5th scale degree (F#-A#-C#-E). Play scale starting an Aug 4th above chord's root.

Here are two ways to think about the Arabian Major 3rd mode:
1-Compare it to other scales. For example:

C Locrian	C	Db	**Eb**	**F**	Gb	Ab	Bb	C
C Arabian Major Mode 3	C	Db	**Ebb**	**Fb**	Gb	Ab	Bb	C
C Chromatic Scale	C	Db	D					
C Whole Tone Scale	C		D		E	Gb	Ab	Bb	C
C Arabian Major Mode 3	C	Db	D		E	Gb	Ab	Bb	C

2-Think of the intervals or half-steps between each scale degree.

For example: C Arabian 3rd mode:	E	F	Gb	Ab	Bb	C	D	E
	1	1	2	2	2	2	2	

Here are the 12 Arabian Major 3rd modes: [min 2nd]
                         [min 2nd]

C	Db	Ebb	Fb	Gb	Ab	Bb	C
C#	D	Eb	F	G	A	B	C#
D	Eb	Fb	Gb	Ab	Bb	C	D
Eb	E	F	G	A	B	C#	Eb
E	F	Gb	Ab	Bb	C	D	E
F	F#	G	A	B	C#	D#	F
F#	G	Ab	Bb	C	D	E	F#
G	Ab	Bbb	Cb	Db	Eb	F	G
G#	A	Bb	C	D	E	F#	G#
A	Bb	Cb	Db	Eb	F	G	A
Bb	B	C	D	E	F#	G#	Bb
B	C	Db	Eb	F	G	A	B

Half-steps between notes:
1-1-2-2-2-2-2

whole tones

Pg. 79

Two Semitone Tritone Scale

A six-note scale (Hexatonic) with two 3-note chromatics separated by 4 half-steps.
It's a symmetrical scale, following the same half-step pattern of 1-1-4-1-1-4.
It divides the octave into even sections.

    Example: C   Db   D   F#   G   Ab

Interesting or defining features:
Two clusters of 3 semitones separated by Major 3rds (4 half-steps).
The lowest notes of each of the 3 note clusters are a tritone apart (6 half-steps).

Chords that may be used with this scale: (examples in C)
Dominant 7(b5) chord (D-F#-Ab-C) built on 3rd scale degree.
Major 7 sus 4 chord built on 2nd scale degree (Db-Gb-Ab-C).

Here are two ways to think about the Two Semitone Tritone scale:
1-Think of its intervals or half steps

    For example: C   Db   D   F#   G   Ab   C
                              1   1   4   1   1   4

2-Think of chromatic clusters and Major 3rd between. For example:

    C Two Semitone Tritone scale: C Db D   F# G Ab   C
                                      half-steps M3 half-steps M3
                                (M3=Major 3rd or 4 half-steps)

Here are the 12 Two Semitone Tritone scales:

Half-steps between notes:
1-1-4-1-1-4

C	Db	D	F#	G	Ab	C
C#	D	Eb	G	G#	A	C#
D	Eb	E	G#	A	A#	D
Eb	E	F	A	A#	B	Eb
E	F	F#	A#	B	C	E
F	Gb	G	B	C	Db	F
Gb	G	Ab	C	Db	D	Gb
G	Ab	A	Db	D	Eb	G
Ab	A	Bb	D	D#	E	Ab
A	Bb	B	D#	E	F	A
Bb	B	C	E	F	Gb	Bb
B	C	C#	F	Gb	G	B

Copyright 2013 by Kevin G. Pace
PaceMusicServices.com

Major Tetrachord Octatonic Scale

An eight note scale made up of two major tetrachords separated by a half-step.
A tetrachord is made up of 2 whole steps followed by a half step.
A tetrachord is like the first 4 notes of a major scale.

Example:

C	D	E	F	F#	G#	A#	B
1st 4 notes of C Major				1st 4 notes of F# Major			

Interesting or defining features:
Minor 2nds between scale degrees 3 & 4, 4 & 5, 7 & 8, and 8 & 1

Some chords that may be used with this scale: (examples in C)
Dominant 7 (#5) (C-E-G#-Bb)   Augmented Major 7 (C-E-G#-B)
Dominant 7 (b5) (C-E-Gb-Bb)   Dominant 9 (#5) (C-E-G#-Bb-D)
Dominant 9 (b5) (C-E-Gb-Bb-D)

Here are two ways to think about the Major Tetrachord Octatonic Scale:
1-Think of its intervals or half-steps

For example:

C	D	E	F	F#	G#	A#	B	C
2	2	1	1	2	2	1	1	

2-Play the first 4 notes of a major scale, then play the first 4 notes of a major scale up a diminished 5th or an augmented 4th (6 half-steps) from the start note of the 1st half scale.

Example:
C Major (1st tetrachord):   C   D   E   F
F# Major (1st tetrachord):   F#   G#   A#   B

Here are the 12 Major Tetrachord Octatonic Scales

Half-steps between notes:
2-2-1-1-2-2-1-1

C	D	E	F	F#	G#	A#	B	C
Db	Eb	F	Gb	G	A	B	C	Db
D	E	F#	G	Ab	Bb	C	Db	D
Eb	F	G	Ab	A	B	C#	D	Eb
E	F#	G#	A	Bb	C	D	Eb	E
F	G	A	Bb	B	C#	D#	E	F
F#	G#	A#	B	C	D	E	F	F#
G	A	B	C	Db	Eb	F	Gb	G
Ab	Bb	C	Db	D	E	F#	G	Ab
A	B	C#	D	Eb	F	G	Ab	A
Bb	C	D	Eb	E	F#	G#	A	Bb
B	C#	D#	E	F	G	A	Bb	B

Copyright 2013 by Kevin G. Pace
PaceMusicServices.com

Tri-Cluster Nonatonic Scale

A nine note scale made up of three, three-note sets of semitones, separated by a whole step.

Example: C C# D E F F# G# A Bb

Interesting or defining features:
Follows a repeating pattern of half-step, half-step, whole-step repeated three times within an octave.

Some chords that may be used with this scale: (examples in C)
Dominant 7(#5) (C-E-G#-Bb)
Dominant 7(b5) (C-E-Gb-Bb)

Here are two ways to think about the Tri-Cluster Nonatonic Scale:
1-Think of its intervals or half-steps
   For example:

   C C# D E F F# G# A Bb C
   1   1 2 1 1   2 1   1 2

2-Play the first 3 notes of a chromatic scale, skip up 2 half-steps, play 3 more notes from the chromatic scale, keep repeating this pattern.
   Example:
      3 chromatics: C   C#   D
      3 chromatics: E   F   F#
      3 chromatics: G#   A   Bb

Here are the 12 Tri-Cluster Nonatonic Scales:

		min 2nd			min 2nd			min 2nd		
	min 2nd			min 2nd			min 2nd			
	C	C#	D	E	F	F#	G#	A	Bb	C
	C#	D	Eb	F	F#	G	A	Bb	B	C#
Half-steps between notes:	D	Eb	E	F#	G	Ab	Bb	B	C	D
2-2-1-1-2-2-1-1	Eb	E	F	G	Ab	A	B	C	Db	Eb
	E	F	F#	Ab	A	Bb	C	Db	D	E
	F	F#	G	A	Bb	B	C#	D	Eb	F
	F#	G	Ab	Bb	B	C	D	Eb	E	F#
	G	Ab	A	B	C	Db	Eb	E	F	G
	G#	A	Bb	C	Db	D	E	F	F#	G#
	A	Bb	B	C#	D	Eb	F	F#	G	A
	Bb	B	C	D	Eb	E	F#	G	Ab	Bb
	B	C	Db	Eb	E	F	G	G#	A	B

Decatonic Scale

This ten tone scale is symmetrical.
It is made up of 5 chromatic tones followed by a whole step. This pattern repeats.

Example: C   C#   D   D#   E   F#   G   G#   A   Bb

Interesting or defining features:
Follows a repeating pattern of H-H-H-H-W repeated twice within an octave.
(H=Half-step, W=Whole step)

Since this scale has all but two tones, many chords can be formed within this scale.

Some chords that may be used with this scale: (examples in C)

Dominant 7 (C-E-G-Bb)	Minor 7 (C-Eb-G-Bb)
Dominant 7(#5) (C-E-G#-Bb)	Fully diminished 7 (C-Eb-Gb-A)
Dominant 7(b5) (C-E-Gb-Bb)	Half diminished 7 (C-Eb-Gb-Bb)

Here are two ways to think about the Decatonic scale:

1-Think of its intervals or half-steps

For example:

C	C#	D	D#	E	F#	G	G#	A	Bb	C
	1	1	1	1	2	1	1	1	1	2

2-Play the first 5 notes of a chromatic scale, skip up 2 half-steps, play 5 more notes from the chromatic scale.

Example:

5 chromatics: C   C#   D   D#   E
5 chromatics: F#   G   G#   A   Bb

Here are the 12 Decatonic Scales:

Half-steps between notes:
2-2-1-1-2-2-1-1

				Whole Tone					
C	C#	D	D#	E	F#	G	G#	A	Bb	C
C#	D	Eb	E	F	G	Ab	A	Bb	B	C#
D	Eb	E	F	F#	Ab	A	Bb	B	C	D
Eb	E	F	F#	G	A	Bb	B	C	Db	Eb
E	F	F#	G	Ab	Bb	B	C	Db	D	E
F	F#	G	Ab	A	B	C	Db	D	Eb	F
F#	G	Ab	A	Bb	C	Db	D	Eb	E	F#
G	Ab	A	Bb	B	Db	D	Eb	E	F	G
G#	A	Bb	B	C	D	Eb	E	F	F#	G#
A	Bb	B	C	Db	Eb	E	F	F#	G	A
Bb	B	C	Db	D	E	F	F#	G	Ab	Bb
B	C	Db	D	Eb	F	F#	G	G#	A	B
Chromatic					Chromatic				

Copyright 2013 by Kevin G. Pace
PaceMusicServices.com

Scales to Play with chords

See individual scale pages for further explanation. There are other chords, but these are some of the more common ones.

Chord	Scales	Chord spelling in C	Possible 1 hand chord voicing	Bi-chordal voicing
Altered chords (a Dominant 7 chord with any combination of b5, #5, b9, and/or #9). See several of the dominant 7 chords listed below.	Octatonic (half-whole) Altered Scale (Note: If you combine all the notes of all possible altered chords, you end up with a chromatic scale. So any note will work with an altered dominant 7 chord.)	C7(b5) = C-E-Gb-Bb C7(#5) = C-E-G#-Bb C7(b5,b9) = C-E-Gb-Bb-Db C7(#5,b9) = C-E-G#-Bb-Db C7(#5,#9) = C-E-G#-Bb-D# C7(b5,#9) = C-E-Gb-Bb-D#, etc.		NA
Any & all chords	Chromatic Scale (pg. 47)	NA	NA	NA
Augmented Major 13(#11)	Lydian Augmented (pg. 23)	C-E-G#-B-D-F#-A	C, then D-F#-G#-A	D Triad C Aug Maj 7
Augmented Major 7 Also called Major 7(#5)	Gypsy M3 above chord's root (pg. 48) Harmonic Major (pg. 37) Ionian #5 (pg. 31) Lydian Augmented (pg. 23) Lydian Augmented #2 (pg. 42) Lydian Augmented Major 7 Pent (pg. 60) Lydian Augmented (add 9) Pent (pg. 62) Major Pent(b6) M3 above chord's root (pg. 56) Major Tetrachord Octatonic (pg. 80) Persian (pg. 52) Phrygian b4 (pg. 39) Symmetrical Augmented (pg. 46) Whole Tone (pg. 20)	C-E-G#-B	C-E-G#-B --------------------- (On chords below, use pedal to sustain the root or you may even omit the root)	
Augmented Dominant 7	see Dominant 7(#5)			
Augmented Major 7(#9)	Altered (pg. 27) Major Pent(b3) m2 above chord's root (pg. 57)	C-E-G#-B-D#	Play C, then E-G#-B-D#	G#m Triad C Aug Triad
Diminished, Fully (Fully-diminished 7)	Altered b7 (pg. 35) Diminished (add 11) Pentatonic (pg. 66) Diminished 9 Pentatonic (pg. 65) Dim Major 7 Pentatonic (pg. 68) Diminished (#5) Pentatonic (pg. 67) Dorian #4 (pg. 32) Locrian b7 (pg. 43) Octatonic whole-half (pg. 45)	C-Eb-Gb-A	C-Eb-Gb-A	
Diminished, Half (Half-diminished 7)	Altered (pg. 27) Decatonic (pg. 82) Dorian b5 (pg. 38) Half-dim Pent (add 4) (pg. 59) Half diminished 9 Pentatonic (pg. 63) Half diminished b13 Pentatonic (pg. 64) Locrian (pg. 9) Locrian #2 (pg. 26) Locrian #6 (30) Minor 6 (add 4) Pent a m3 above chord's root (pg. 58) Minor Pent (mode 1) a M2 below root (pg. 11) Minor Pent (mode 1) a P4 above root (pg. 11) Phrygian #3 a P4 above chord's root (pg. 33)	C-Eb-Gb-Bb	C-Eb-Gb-Bb	

Chord	Scales	Chord spelling in C	Possible 1 hand chord voicing	Bi-chordal voicing
Diminished (Half-diminished 9)	Decatonic (pg. 82) Dorian #4 (pg. 32) Dorian b5 (pg. 38) Half-diminished 9 Pentatonic (pg. 63) Half-dim b13 Pentatonic (pg. 64) Locrian #2 (pg. 26) Minor Pent a m3 above chord's root (pg. 11)	C-Eb-Gb-Bb-D	C, Eb-Gb-Bb-D	Gb Aug C dim Triad
Diminished (Half-diminished 11)	Locrian #2 (pg. 26)	C-Eb-Gb-Bb-F	C, Gb-Bb-(Eb)-F	
Diminished Major 7	Diminished Major 7 Pentatonic (pg. 68) Octatonic (whole-half) (pg. 45)	C-Eb-Gb-B	C-Eb-Gb-B	
Diminished triad	Dorian b5 (pg. 38) Locrian #6 (pg. 30) (Also see fully diminished below)	C-Eb-Gb	C-Eb-Gb	
Dominant 7	Aeolian b4 (pg. 74) Altered (pg. 27) Arabian Major mode 3 (pg. 78) Arab Maj mode 3 an Aug 4 abv chord's root (pg. 78) Bebop 7th (pg. 16) Blues Major (pg. 19) Blues minor (pg. 18) Decatonic (pg. 82) Dim(#5) Pent, M3 above chord's root (pg. 67) Dim 9 Pent, M2 below chord's root (pg. 65) Dim(add 11) Pent, P5 abv chord's root (pg. 66) Dim Maj 7 Pent, m2 above chord's root (pg. 68) Dominant 9 Pentatonic (pg. 69) Dorian #4 a M2 below chord's root (pg. 32) Half-dim b13 Pent, M3 abv chord's root (pg. 64) Ionian #5 a M3 below chord's root (pg. 31) Lydian Dominant (pg. 24) Lydian Dominant b2 (pg. 76) Major Pentatonic (mode 2) (pg. 12) Minor Lydian Aug Pent, M3 abv chord's root (pg. 61) Minor Pentatonic (mode 1) (pg. 11) Mixolydian (pg. 7) Mixolydian b2 (pg. 41) Mixolydian b6 (pg. 25) Octatonic half-whole (pg. 45) Phrygian #3 (pg. 33) Phrygian b4 (pg. 39) Symmetrical Augmented (pg. 46)	C-E-G-Bb	C-E-G-Bb	
Dominant 7(#5) (Augmented Dom 7)	Altered (pg. 27) Arabian Major (pg. 49) Locrian #3 (pg. 54) Octatonic (half-whole) (pg. 45) Phrygian b4 (pg. 39) Whole Tone (pg. 20)	C-E-G#-Bb	C-E-G#-Bb	
Dominant 7(#5/#9) (Augmented Dom 7(#9))	Altered (pg. 27) Major Pent (mode 2) Aug 4 above root (pt. 12) Major Pent b3 a m2 above chord's root (pg. 57) Octatonic (half-whole) (pg. 45)	C-E-G#-Bb-D#	C, E-G#-Bb-D#	Ab Triad C7 (no 5)

Chord	Scales	Chord spelling in C	Possible 1 hand chord voicing	Bi-chordal voicing
Dominant 7(#9)	Altered (pg. 27) Minor Blues (pg. 18) Minor Pentatonic (pg. 11) Octatonic (half-whole) (pg. 45) Phrygian b4 (pg. 39)	C-E-G-Bb-D#	C, E-G-Bb-D#	
Dominant 7(#9, #11)	Altered (pg. 27) Minor Blues (pg. 18)	C-E-G-Bb-D#-F#	C, Bb-D#-F#	Ebm Triad C7
Dominant 7(#9/b5)	Altered (pg. 27) Major Pent (mode 2) Aug 4 above root (pt. 12) Octatonic (half-whole) (pg. 45)	C-E-Gb-Bb-D#	C, E-Gb-Bb-D#	Ebm Triad C7(b5)
Dominant 7(#11)	Altered (pg. 27) Lydian-Dominant (pg. 24) Octatonic (half-whole) (pg. 45)	C-E-G-Bb-F#	C, Bb-E-F#	
Dominant 7(b5)	Altered (pg. 27) Arabian Major (pgs. 49, 78) Decatonic (pg. 82) Locrian #3 (pg. 54) Lydian Dominant (pg. 24) Lydian Dominant b2 (pg. 76) Major Tetrachord Octatonic (pg. 80) Octatonic (half-whole) (pg. 45) Tri-Cluster Nonatonic (pg. 81) Two Semitone Tritone a M2 below chord's root (pg. 79) Whole Tone (pg. 20)	C-E-Gb-Bb	C-E-Gb-Bb	
Dominant 7(b9)	Altered (pg. 27) Dim(#5) Pent, M3 above chord's root (pg. 67) Dim 9 Pent, M2 below chord's root (pg. 65) Dim(add 11) Pent, P5 abv chord's root (pg. 66) Dim Maj 7 Pent, m2 above chord's root (pg. 68) Half-dim b13 Pent, M3 abv chord's root (pg. 64) Mixolydian b2 (pg. 41) Octatonic (half-whole) (pg. 45)	C-E-G-Bb-Db	C, E-G-Bb-Db	
Dominant 7(b9/#5)	Altered (pg. 27) Locrian #3 (pg. 54) Major Pent, Aug 4 above chord's root (pg. 12)	C-E-G#-Bb-Db	C, E-G#-Bb-Db	
Dominant 7(b9/b5)	Altered (pg. 27) Locrian #3 (pg. 54) Major Pent, Aug 4 above chord's root (pg. 12) Octatonic (half-whole) (pg. 45)	C-E-Gb-Bb-Db	C, E-Gb-Bb-Db	Gb Triad C7(b5)
Dominant 7(b9, b13)	Altered (pg. 27) Ionian #5 a M3 below chord's root (pg. 31) Major Pent (mode 2) on b9, b5, or #5 (pg. 12) Phrygian #3 (pg. 33) Phrygian b4 (pg. 39)	C-E-G-Bb-Db-Ab	C, Bb-Db-E-Ab	C#m Triad C7
Dominant 7(b13)	Altered (pg. 27) Mixolydian b6 (pg. 25) Whole tone (pg. 20)	C-E-G-Bb-Ab	C, Bb-E-G-Ab	

Chord	Scales	Chord spelling in C	Possible 1 hand chord voicing	Bi-chordal voicing
Dominant 7sus4	Dorian b5 a P5 above chord's root (pg. 38) Mixolydian (pg. 7) Mixolydian b6 (pg. 25) Pent 3 (pg. 13) Pent 3 a P5 above chord's root (pg. 13) Pent 4 a M2 above chord's root (pg. 14) Pent 5 a P4 above chord's root (pg.15) Phrygian #3 (pg. 33)	C-F-G-Bb	C-F-G-Bb	
Dominant 7sus4(b9)	Phrygian (pg. 5) Phrygian b4 (pg. 39)	C-F-G-Bb-Db	C, F-G-Bb-Db	
Dominant 9	Bebop 7th (pg. 16) Blues Major (pg. 19) Dominant 9 Pent (pg. 69) Major Pent (mode 2) (pg. 12) Major Pent a P4 above chord's root (pg. 12) Mixolydian (pg. 7)	C-E-G-Bb-D	C, E-G-Bb-D	
Dominant 9(#5)	Major Tetrachord Octatonic (pg. 80) Whole Tone (pg. 20)	C-E-G#-Bb-D	C, E-G#-Bb-D	
Dominant 9(#5/#11) or Aug 9(#11)	Whole Tone (pg. 20)	C-E-G#-Bb-D-F#	C, G#-Bb-D-F#	Bb Aug C Aug
Dominant 9(b5)	Lydian Dominant (pg. 24) Major Tetrachord Octatonic (pg. 80) Whole Tone (pg. 20)	C-E-Gb-Bb-D	C, E-Gb-Bb-D	
Dominant 9 sus	Major Pent a M2 below chord's root (pg. 12) Pentatonic Mode 3 (pg. 13)	C-F-G-Bb-D	C, F-G-Bb-D	
Dominant 9(#11)	Half-diminished 9 Pentatonic (pg. 63) Lydian Dominant (pg. 24)	C-E-G-Bb-D-F#	C, Bb-D-E-F#	Bb Aug C Triad
Dominant 13	Bebop 7th (pg. 16) Dominant 9 Pentatonic (pg. 69) Major Pentatonic (mode 2) (pg. 12) Mixolydian (pg. 7)	C-E-G-Bb-D-F-A	C, Bb-D-E-A	Dm Triad C7
Dominant 13 sus	Major Pent a P4 above chord's root (pg. 12)	C-F-G-Bb-D-A	C, Bb-D-F-A	Dm Triad C7 shell*
Dominant 13(#11)	Bebop 7th (pg. 16) Dominant 9 Pent (pg. 69) Lydian Dominant (pg. 24) Major Pentatonic (mode 2) (pg. 12) Major Pent (b6) M2 above chord's root (pg. 56) Mixolydian (pg. 7)	C-E-G-Bb-D-F#-A	C, Bb-D-F#-A	D Triad C7
Dominant 13(#9)	Major Blues (pg. 19) Octatonic (half-whole) (pg. 45)	C-E-G-Bb-D#-F-A	C, Bb-D#-G-A	
Dominant 13(b9)	Mixolydian b2 (pg. 41) Octatonic (half-whole) (pg. 45)	C-E-G-Bb-Db-F-A	C, Bb-Db-E-A	Db Aug C7
Dominant 13(b9, #11)	Lydian Dominant b2 (pg. 76)	C-E-G-Bb-Db-F#-A	C, Bb-Db-E-F#-A	F#m inv 2 C7
Full & half diminished 7, 9, 11	see Diminished chords	NA	NA	
Lydian Augmented Major 7	Lydian Augmented (add 9) Pentatonic (pg. 62)	C-F#-G#-B	C-F#-G#-B	
Lydian Augmented Major 9	Lydian Augmented (add 9) Pentatonic (pg. 62)	C-F#-G#-B-D	C D-F#-G#-B	

Chord	Scales	Chord spelling in C	Possible 1 hand chord voicing	Bi-chordal voicing
Major 6	Bebop Major (pg. 17) Blues Major (pg. 19) Ionian (pg. 3) Lydian Dominant (pg. 24) Pentatonic 1 starting on 6th of the chord (pg. 11) Pentatonic 2 (pg. 12) Pent 3 starting a M2 above chord's root (pg. 13) Pent 4 starting a M3 above chord's root (pg. 14) Pent 5 starting a P5 up from chord's root (pg. 15)	C-E-G-A	C-E-G-A	
Major b6	Harmonic Major (pg. 37) Major Pentatonic b6 (pg. 56)	C-E-G-Ab	C-E-G-Ab	
Major 7	Bebop Major (pg. 17) East Indian Purvi (pg. 53) Gypsy (pg. 48) Harmonic Major (pg. 37) Ionian (pg. 3) Ionian b2 (pg. 73) Lydian (pg. 6) Lydian #2 (pg. 34) Major Pentatonic (mode 2) (pg. 12) Major Pent a M2 or P5 above chord's root (pg. 12) Pelog Pent a M3 above chord's root (pg. 70) Symmetrical Augmented (pg. 46)	C-E-G-B	C-E-G-B	
Major 7(#5)	See Augmented Major 7	NA	NA	
Major 7(#11)	Harmonic Major (pg. 37) Lydian (pg. 6) Lydian #2 (pg. 34) Major Pent a M2 above chord's root (pg. 12)	C-E-G-B-F#	C, B-E-F#	
Major 7(b9)	Ionian b2 (pg. 73) Lydian #2 (pg. 34)	C-E-G-B-Db	C, G-B-Db-E	
Major 7(b5)	Lydian (pg. 6) Lydian #2 (pg. 34) Major Pent (mode 2) a M2 above root (pg. 12) Persian (pg. 52) Phrygian a m2 below chord's root (pg. 5) Phrygian #3 a m2 below chord's root (pg. 33) Phrygian b4 a m2 below chord's root (pg. 39)	C-E-Gb-B	C-E-Gb-B	
Major 7(b13)	Harmonic Major (pg. 37)	C-E-G-Ab-B	C-E-G-Ab-B	
Major 7 sus 4	Two Semitone Tritone m2 below root (pg. 79)	C-F-G-B	C-F-G-B	
Major 9	Harmonic Major (pg. 37) Ionian (pg. 3) Lydian (pg. 6) Lydian #2 (pg. 34) Major Pent a M2 above chord's root (pg. 12)	C-E-G-B-D	C, E-G-B-D	
Major 9(#5/#11)	Whole Tone (pg. 20)	C-E-G#-B-D-F#	C, G#-B-D-F#	
Major 9(#11)	Lydian (pg. 6) Lydian #2 (pg. 34) Major Pent a M2 above chord's root (pg. 12)	C-E-G-B-D-F#	C, B-D-E-F#	Bm Triad C Triad
Major 13	Ionian (pg. 3)	C-E-G-B-D-F-A	C, B-D-F-A	Dm Triad C Maj 7

Chord	Scales	Chord spelling in C	Possible 1 hand chord voicing	Bi-chordal voicing
Major 13(#11)	Lydian (pg. 6) Major Pent a M2 above chord's root (pg. 12)	C-E-G-B-D-F#-A	C, B-D-F#-A	D Triad C Maj 7
Minor(add 9) triad	Hirajoshi Pentatonic (pg. 71)	C-D-Eb-G	C, Eb-G-C-D	
Minor 6	Blues Major (pg. 19) Dorian (pg. 4) Dorian #4 (pg. 32) Half-dim (add 4) Pent a m3 below chord's root (pg. 59) Half-dim 9 Pent, m3 below chord's root (pg. 63) Lydian b3 (pg. 40) Melodic Minor (pg. 21) Major Pent b3 (pg. 57) Minor Pent (mode 1) (pg. 11) Minor Pent a M2 above chord's root (pg. 11) Minor 6 (add 4) Pent (pg. 58) Phrygian #6 (pg. 22)	C-Eb-G-A	C-Eb-G-A	
Minor b6	Hirajoshi Pentatonic (pg. 71) Pelog Pentatonic (pg. 70)	C-Eb-G-Ab	C-Eb-G-Ab	
Minor 7	Aeolian (pg. 8) Aeolian b4 (pg. 74) Bebop 7th a P4 above chord's root (pg. 16) Blues minor (pg. 18) Decatonic (pg. 82) Dorian (pg. 4) Dorian #4 (pg. 32) Gypsy a P5 above chord's root (pg. 48) Melodic minor (pg. 21) Minor 6 (add 4) Pent (pg. 58) Minor Pent (mode 1) (pg. 11) Minor Pent (mode 1) up P5 from chord's root Minor Pent (mode 1) up M2 from chord's root Pent 3 a P4 above chord's root (pg. 13) Pent 4 a P5 above the chord's root (pg. 14) Pent 5 a M2 below chord's root (pg. 15) Phrygian (pg. 5) Phrygian #6 (pg. 22) Phrygian b4 (pg. 39)	C-Eb-G-Bb	C-Eb-G-Bb	
Minor 7 sus4(b9)	Phrygian (pg. 5)	C-F-G-Bb-Db	C, F-G-Bb-Db	
Minor 7(#5)	Pentatonic 4 (pg. 14)	C-Eb-G#-Bb	C-Eb-G#-Bb	
Minor 7(b5)	See diminished (half-diminished 7)	C-Eb-Gb-Bb	C-Eb-Gb-Bb	
Minor 9(b11, b13)	Aeolian b4 (pg. 74)	C-Eb-G-Bb-D-Fb-Ab)	C, Bb-Eb-Fb-Ab	Bb7(b5) C mi triad
Minor 9	Aeolian (pg. 8) Dorian (pg. 4) Minor Pentatonic (mode 1) (pg. 11) Minor Pent a P5 above chord's root (pg. 11) Minor Pent a M2 above chord's root (pg. 11) Minor 6 (add 4) Pent (pg. 58)	C-Eb-G-Bb-D	C, Eb-G-Bb-D	Gm Triad Cm Triad

Chord	Scales	Chord spelling in C	Possible 1 hand chord voicing	Bi-chordal voicing
Minor 11	Aeolian (pg. 8) Dorian (pg. 4) Minor Pent (pg. 11) Minor Pent a P5 above chord's root (pg. 11) Minor 6 (add 4) Pent (pg. 58)	C-Eb-G-Bb-D-F	C, G-Bb-D-F	Bb Triad Cm Triad
Minor 13	Dorian (pg. 4) Minor Pent a M2 above chord's root (pg 11) Minor 6 (add 4) Pent (pg. 58)	C-Eb-G-Bb-D-F-A	C, Bb-D-F-A	Dm Triad Cm7
Minor Major 7	Arabian Major mode 3 a m2 below chord's root (pg. 78) Gypsy starting on 5th of the chord (pg. 48) Harmonic Minor (pg. 29) Harmonic Minor b2 (pg. 50) Hungarian Gypsy (pg. 51) Lydian b3 (pg. 40) Major Pent(b6) a P4 below chord's root (pg. 56) Melodic minor (pg. 21) Phrygian #6 a M2 above chord's root (pg. 22) Symmetrical Augmented (pg. 46)	C-Eb-G-B	C-Eb-G-B	
Minor Major 7 (#5)	Minor Lydian Augmented Pentatonic (pg. 61)	C-Eb-G#-B	C-Eb-G#-B	
Minor Major 7 (b5) (See Dim Major 7)	Lydian b3 (pg. 40)	C-Eb-Gb-B	C-Eb-Gb-B	
Minor Major 9	Harmonic Minor (pg. 29) Melodic Minor (pg. 21)	C-Eb-G-B-D	C, Eb-G-B-D	G Triad Cm Triad
Sus triad	Pentatonic 5 (pg. 15)	C-F-G	C-F-G	

*Shell = outside notes of chord only. For example, the shell of C7 = C-Bb

Notes: Since the modes of the various parent scales consist of the same notes, any chord that goes with one mode will therefore go with another. For example:

C Melodic Minor (the parent mode)   =   C-D-Eb-F-G-A-B-C

D Phrygian #6 (2nd mode of Melodic Minor) = D-Eb-F-G-A-B-C-D

These two scales use the same notes, just in a different order. So since a C minor-Major 7 chord will work with C Melodic Minor, it will also work with D Phrygian #6 and all of the modes of Melodic Minor. Since a D minor 7 chord will work with D Phrygian #6, then it will work with C Melodic Minor and all the other modes of Melodic minor. This same generalization applies to all parent scales and their respective modes. Some experimenting with this idea can lead to some interesting chord-scale combinations.

More on Major Pentatonic (mode 2) and chords (see pg. 12)

If the V7 chord in a ii, V, I progression is *unaltered* then use the following:

Major Pentatonic built on root of the I chord: Examples:
- ii   Play a minor 7 chord a M2 above the scale's tonic   Dm7 with C Major Pent
- V   Play a Dominant 7 chord a P5 above scale's tonic   G7 with C Major Pent
- I   Play a Major 7 chord on scale's tonic   C Maj7 with C Major Pent

or

Major Pentatonic built on root of the V chord: Examples:
- ii   Play a minor 7 chord a P4 below the scale's tonic   Dm7 with G Major Pent
- V   Play a Dominant 7 chord on the scale's tonic   G7 with G Major Pent
- I   Play a Major 7 chord a P5 below scale's tonic   C Maj7 with G Major Pent

If the V7 chord in a ii, V, I progression is *altered* then use the following:
- ii   Play a minor 7 chord a M2 above scale's tonic   Dm7 with C Major Pent
- V   Play a Dom 7 altered chord a tritone above scale's tonic   G7 alt with Db Major Pent
- I   Play a Major 7 chord on scale's tonic   C Maj7 with C Major Pent

or

- ii   Play a minor 7 chord a P4 below scale's tonic   Dm7 with G Major Pent
- V   Play a Dom 7 altered chord a tritone above scale's tonic   G7 alt with Db Major Pent
- I   Play a Major 7 chord a P5 below scale's tonic   C Maj7 with G Major Pent

For more information, see:
Scott D. Reeves, *Creative Jazz Improvisation*, 4th ed. New Jersey: Pearson/Prentice Hall, 2007, pgs. 290-291.

More on Minor Pentatonic (mode 1) and chords (see pg. 11)

	Examples:
Play a minor 7 chord on the scale's tonic	Cm7 chord with C Minor Pent
This is best when playing in a minor key.	
Play a minor 7 chord a P5 above scale's tonic	Cm7 chord with G Minor Pent
This is best when the chord is a ii chord in a major key.	
Play a minor 7 chord a M2 below the scale's tonic	Cm7 chord with D Minor Pent
This is best when the chord is a ii chord in a major key.	
Play a half-diminished 7 chord a whole step above the scale's tonic	Cm7(b5) chord with Bb Minor Pent
Play a half-diminished 7 chord a Perfect 4th below the scale's tonic	Cm7(b5) chord with F Minor Pent

For more information, see:
Scott D. Reeves, *Creative Jazz Improvisation*, 4th ed. New Jersey: Pearson/Prentice Hall, 2007, pgs. 292-293.

Glossary of terms

Augmented 2nd: An interval of 3 half steps. For example between C and D# is an Augmented 2nd. The Augmented 2nd interval occurs in Harmonic Minor and Harmonic Major scales and their modes.

Augmented chord: A triad consisting of two stacked Major 3rds. For example, a D Augmented chord is D-F#-A#. It's the same as a major triad with a raised (sharped) top note.

Chords: Generally, notes stacked in a series of 3rds are called chords. For example, the notes C-E-G are each a 3rd apart. These three notes together are called a C Major chord. The notes D-F#-A-C are each a 3rd apart. These notes together make a D7 chord. The notes E-G-B-D-F# together make an E minor 9 chord (Em9). An exception is the 6 chord such as C-D-G-A. The added 6th is obviously not a stacked 3rd, but is often found in music.

Church Modes: Dorian, Phrygian, Lydian, Mixolydian, Aeolian, Locrian, and Ionian are sometimes called the church modes.

Diminished chord (dim): A triad consisting of two stacked minor 3rds. For example, a C diminished chord is C-Eb-Gb.

Double flat: Lowering a note by two half steps. Written as two flats (bb). For example, Bbb is the same as an A natural.

Double sharp: Raising a note by two half steps. Written as "x". For example Fx is the same as G natural.

Enharmonic spelling: A way of saying that one note can be spelled in more than one way. For example, C# is the same as Db when played on the piano.

Flat: Lowering a note by one half step.

Interval: Distance betweeen two notes.

Major 2nd: An interval of two half steps. For example between C and D is a Major 2nd. Between E and F# is a Major 2nd.

Major 3rd: An interval of four half steps. In a major scale, from scale degree 1 to scale degree 3 is a major 3rd.

Major triad (or chord): Three notes stacked with a Major 3rd on bottom and minor 3rd on top. For example, an Ab Major chord is Ab-C-Eb. Chords are normally spelled by skipping one letter of the alphabet between each note.

Minor 2nd: An interval of one half step. For example between C# and D is a minor 2nd. This is the smallest interval on the piano.

Minor 3rd: An interval of three half steps. In a minor scale, from scale degree 1 to scale degree 3 is a minor 3rd.

Minor chord: Three notes stacked with a minor 3rd on bottom and Major 3rd on top. For example, an Ab minor chord is Ab-Cb-Eb. Chords are normally spelled by skipping one letter of the alphabet between each note. So, even though Cb is the same as B, the Ab minor chord would be spelled with Cb as the middle note.

Modes: Inversions of a scale. For example the C Major scale is C-D-E-F-G-A-B-C. The 2nd mode of C Major is D Dorian which is D-E-F-G-A-B-C-D (C Major starting and ending on D). Often the terms mode and scale are used interchangeably.

Parent mode: The scale from which other modes or scales are derived. For example, the major scale (Ionian) is the parent mode of Dorian, Phrygian, Lydian, Mixolydian, Aeolian, and Locrian. For example, C Major (Ionian) is C-D-E-F-G-A-B-C. D Dorian uses the same notes as C Major, but starting on the 2nd degree of the scale. So D Dorian is D-E-F-G-A-B-C-D. Dorian is the 2nd mode of the Major scale. Here is another example: G Major is G-A-B-C-D-E-F#-G. B Phrygian uses the same notes as G Major, but starting on the 3rd note of the scale. So B Phrygian is B-C-D-E-F#-G-A-B. Phrygian is the 3rd mode of Major. The Major scale is the parent mode.

Perfect 4th (P4): In a major or minor scale, from scale degree 1 to scale degree 4 is a perfect 4th. It is 5 half-steps. A perfect 4th inverted becomes a perfect 5th.

Perfect 5th (P5): In a major or minor scale, from scale degree 1 to scale degree 5 is a perfect 5th. It is 7 half-steps. A perfect 5th inverted becomes a perfect 4th.

Root: The lowest note of a chord in its main position (its root positiion). For example, in a C Major chord (C-E-G), the C is the root of the chord. If you invert the chord (such as E-G-C), C is still the root because it is still a C Major triad. The first note of a scale is sometimes called the root, but it should actually be called the Tonic or scale degree number 1.

Scales: A set of notes that divides an octave in a certain way. Most common scales divide the octave into seven parts. Scales are sometimes called modes.

Sharp: Raising a note by one half step.

Sus: An abbreviation for suspended chord. Generally refers to the 3rd of a chord being moved to the 4th. For example: C Dominant 7 = C-E-G-Bb, and C7 Sus = C-F-G-Bb. Sometimes it is written as sus4. There is also the possibility of a sus 2 chord where the 3rd of a chord is moved to the 2nd. For example: Csus2 = C-D-G.

Tonic: The first note of a scale.

Triad: A three note chord. Triads are often referred to as chords, but since a chord can be more than 3 notes, the word triad is more accurate.

Copyright 2013 by Kevin G. Pace
PaceMusicServices.com

Acknowledgements

Credit needs to be given to those who have taught me, or from whom I have learned.

My inspiration to start this project was Russell Schmidt, head of the Jazz department at the University of Utah. Professor Schmidt is an amazingly talented and knowledgeable person. He opened my eyes to the remarkable world of musical scales.

Two books were also quite helpful to reference. These are:

The Jazz Language, A Theory Text for Jazz Composition and Improvisation, by Dan Haerle.

Creative Jazz Improvisation by Scott D. Reeves.

Additional Reading

For more information on Chords see: *The Comprehensive Book of Chords for Piano & Keyboard Players* by Kevin G. Pace. Available on Amazon.com or PaceMusicServices.com.

Printed in Poland
by Amazon Fulfillment
Poland Sp. z o.o., Wrocław